PRAISE

HABIT

PRAISE

FINDING GOD IN SUNSETS AND SUSHI

HABIT

DAVID CROWDER

NAVPRESS
Discipleship Inside Out™

NavPress is the publishing ministry of The Navigators, an international Christian organization and leader in personal spiritual development. NavPress is committed to helping people grow spiritually and enjoy lives of meaning and hope through personal and group resources that are biblically rooted, culturally relevant, and highly practical.

**For a free catalog go to www.NavPress.com
or call 1.800.366.7788 in the United States or 1.800.839.4769 in Canada.**

NAVPRESS, the NAVPRESS logo, TH1NK and the TH1NK logo are registered trademarks of NavPress. Absence of ® in connection with marks of NavPress or other parties does not indicate an absence of registration of those marks. An absence of vitamin A can be an indicator of an absence of proper dietary nutrition.

ISBN 13: 978-1-57683-670-5

Cover design by Disciple Design
Cover photograph by Gary Walpole
United States 2004 Summer Olympics Archery Team: Janet Dykman, Jennifer Nichols, Stephanie White-Arnold, Butch Johnson, John Magera, Vic Wunderle

Unless otherwise identified, all Scripture quotations in this publication are taken from The Message Remix, copyright © 2003, used by permission of NavPress Publishing Group. Other versions used include: the HOLY BIBLE: NEW INTERNATIONAL VERSION® (NIV®). Copyright © 1973, 1978, 1984 by International Bible Society. Used by permission of Zondervan Publishing House. All rights reserved. Unless otherwise identified, all hummus references are taken from a conversation I had in 2003 and are in fact references to hummus, the food that "renders all others obsolete." (A direct quote from my friend Mike stated to me while eating hummus and crackers in Denver at a table out-of-doors under an umbrella in the sunlight.) Unfortunately, there are no hummus references in this book, but it should still be kept readily in mind.

Crowder, David.
   Praise habit : finding God in sunsets and sushi / David Crowder.
      p. cm.
   Includes bibliographical references.
   ISBN 1-57683-670-3
   1. Bible. O.T. Psalms--Meditations. 2. Praise of God--Meditations.
   I. Title.
   BS1430.54.C76 2004
   242'.5--dc22
                              2004022963

Printed in the United States of America

Please circle a number from 3–10 indicating your bias toward penguins: 3 being a very strong dislike or burgeoning revulsion, and a 10 representative of an unrequited love. For reference, I am at about a 7.4.

9 10 11 12 13 14 / 16 15 14 13 12 11

Penguin—docile, devious, calculating, ability to fly

In Memoriam:
Sandra Mauldin Pynes (1959–1999)

CONTENTS

ACKNOWLEDGMENTS

Thank you, Toni, Gabe Filkey, Steve Parolini, Terry Behimer, Amy Spencer, Cara Iverson, Pat Miller, all at NavPress, Eugene Peterson, Eric Johnson, Jim Lund, Kyle Lake, Ben and Jamie, all at UBC, Cameron Smith, Shelley, Louie, Carrie, all at Sixstepsrecords, Mike Hogan, Mike Dodson, Jeremy Bush, Jason Solley, Jack Parker, Denise George, Brad Odonnell, Matt Allen, all at EMI/CMG, Mom and Dad, Sandra, Madison, Caitlyn, Jordan.

INTRODUCTION PART 1

Everything in Its Right Place

I used to think I knew where to find God. He seemed to always be where I put Him last.

He was in Sunday school every Sunday morning. He was in "big church" right after. He was there most Sunday nights, too. He was around our dinner table when my father read from the blue Bible-story books. He was there when I prayed before meals. He was there most times I prayed elsewhere, too. He was there during my quiet times. He was at church on Wednesday nights. He was *really* there at summer camp. He loved church camp. I think He just liked summers better in general. Once school started back, the moments with Him were farther spaced, it seems. I enjoyed finding Him. It felt like things were right. Even if they weren't, it felt okay. I wanted more moments with Him. I heard there was a Bible study on Monday nights, so I went, and sure enough—He was there. I had an accountability group and we met on Tuesdays, and sure enough—He was there, too. I heard about another Bible study that met on Thursdays, so I went, and wouldn't you know it, there He was. He began showing up in the songs we sang around 1983. It was called contemporary worship. It was great. He was always in these songs, so I would sing them whenever I wanted to find Him, and sure enough—there He'd be. By the time I got to college I thought I had it all sorted out with everything in its place. Then tragedy came.

Tragedy always comes. If it hasn't come for you, it will. Not the losing-your-homework kind or the having-to-flush-your-goldfish kind, but the kind that leaves you stripped. The kind that tears from you all the ideas about living you once believed untearable. Mine came my junior year of college, and it came in a phone call.

It was my mom. She said, "David, something very terrible has happened." The words that followed were bombs. As they came hurtling toward me through miles of telephone wire, my muscles turned liquid, and when she finished, I was left wilted on the floor, and God was not there. At least I could no longer find Him. And I had no idea where to begin looking again. The places I used to frequent, I no longer trusted. In seven minutes everything I had thought about everything was dramatically different.

College is hard enough without something detonating in the middle of it. It is a pivotal moment. Your values encounter other values in classrooms and textbooks. Your faith is on trial inside libraries and laboratories. In my philosophy classes we read Plato and Aristotle. Aristotle was not a Christian, but he sure sounded like one. This bugged me. Or was it that my Christianity sounded a lot like Aristotle? This possibility was even more troubling. And in literature, thanks to Derrida,[1] deconstruction theory was preventing us from deriving any intended meaning from a text, because apparently language itself was now unstable and arbitrary. In my theology classes we studied how the Scriptures had been assembled, and I was concerned that I had not been informed of this arbitral process earlier in my formation of faith. Had it been hidden from me? Why had I always been given such neat answers for messy questions? Or was this the proper time for the hearing of such things? Perhaps by your junior year of college, after you have been a Christian for fourteen years, you are properly equipped to sort out things like this?

There was a lot of sorting out to be done concerning most things and where they were to be placed in this faith I carried or that was carrying me, and it was proving to be a daunting task. And then in the middle of this sorting, an explosion. I was covered in shrapnel, clotlessly bleeding. And when I had bled out, when there was nothing left, I found Him. And He was not where I thought He was. Nor where I had put Him last.

He was in a Chick-fil-A sandwich.

I have loved Chick-fil-A my whole life. But when your world implodes, nothing tastes good. I was poking at the thing and a thought hit me that there is one part of the sandwich I don't enjoy. There is about a quarter of the breast that consistently dissolves into a lesser grade of meat and soggy breading. I pulled the top bun off and tore the portion away that didn't look appealing. There was a natural break in the meat. It was easily separated. I put the top back on and ate. It was the best chicken sandwich I had ever eaten. I wadded up the foil sandwich bag and smiled for the first time in a really long while.

It may not sound like a real breakthrough, but for me it was truly cathartic. In a small, decisive moment I was aware of what was *good* and took effort to peel away what wasn't and in the process became re-enamored with the Giver of good. I remembered our beginnings, when that statement "It was good" was first uttered. I thought about how the *bad* was never intended. Things started to come to life. Blood that had slowed to a crawl began to find its way through my veins again.

The consequences of this discovery were huge. If He was in a sandwich, where else could He be found? Every moment was becoming holy. Nothing was nonspiritual. This was habitual praise—a perpetually sacred acknowledgment of the Giver of every good thing. A relentless embracing of good and a discarding of bad with an awareness of the one who in the beginning spoke those life-affirming words.

When good is found and we embrace it with abandon, we embrace the Giver of it. This book explores that journey. This book is written in hopes that you begin to find God everywhere. Yes, in church on Sunday at 9:00 a.m., but also in the seemingly mundane. In traffic on Tuesday at 5:15 p.m. In a parent-teacher meeting. In the colors of a sunset. On the other end of a tragic phone call. Every second is an opportunity for praise. There is a choosing to be made. A choosing at each moment. This is the Praise Habit. Finding God moment by revelatory moment, in the sacred and the mundane, in the valley and on the hill, in triumph and tragedy, and living praise erupting because of it. This is what we were made for.

INTRODUCTION PART 2

Your Everyday Ordinary Life

So here's what I want you to do, God helping you: Take your everyday, ordinary life — your sleeping, eating, going-to-work, and walking-around life — and place it before God as an offering. Embracing what God does for you is the best thing you can do for him. Don't become so well-adjusted to your culture that you fit into it without even thinking. Instead, fix your attention on God. You'll be changed from the inside out.

— Romans 12:1-2

8:00 A.M. — *The Alarm Goes Off*

[It is a white, 1940s-style retro clock with the bells on top—inverted silver bowls. A little hammer bangs back and forth between them. It is entirely too loud. A ridiculous volume for such small pieces of metal. I decide this while I knock it to the floor. It stops clanging. . . .]

8:10 A.M. — *The Alarm Goes Off Again*

[I did not know it had this snooze technology when I purchased it. I would have walked away despite its clean lines and green, glow-in-the-dark hands. I mumble something about legitimate 1940s alarm clocks not having such contemporaneous snooze machinery and that this was a lame anachronistic regurgitation of what was once a fine timepiece. I am forced out of bed to stop the clanging, because it was knocked out of reach ten minutes earlier. . . .]

8:12 A.M. — *THE BATHROOM*

[I am now in the bathroom doing what is necessary after a full night of sleep and a fully functioning digestive system. There is no toilet paper. Well, actually there is a small sliver left clinging. I give the piece of paper a gentle tug. I now hold a petite right triangle. I am recalling the hypotenuse-acute angle theorem while doubting that this piece will accommodate my needs. . . .]

8:27 A.M. — *THE YELLING*

[I express my needs at loud volume to my wife, who is downstairs, and wait. . . .]

8:30 A.M. — *THE BRUSHING OF TEETH*

[I brush my teeth. It's a brand-new toothbrush. One of those with bristles of different colors and lengths pointing in all different directions. It looks quite formidable. I would not want to be the spiteful plaque clinging to my teeth with this thing set free. It is a true technological marvel of destruction. It feels sensational. I spit. I am bleeding. I check the box for a warning or for proper-usage instructions. . . .]

8:35 A.M. — *THE DISCARDING OF TRASH*

[I throw the toothbrush away. It is a danger. . . .]

8:36 A.M. — *THE EPIDERMAL CLEANSING*

[I take out a Ponds cleansing towelette to rinse my face. These things are fabulous. I discovered them about a year ago and face cleansing rocketed to new levels of convenience. I observe a blemish just at the point where my right nostril circles and turns into upper lip. I read the Ponds package to make sure I'm doing it right. Maybe the packaged cleansing towelettes are like shampoo in that you should change brands every so often to prevent buildup. Or is the shampoo thing a vicious rumor, one of those urban myths? There is no information regarding any of this on the towelette package. . . .]

8:39 A.M. — *THE CHOOSING OF FASHION*

[I stare into my closet. This can take moments or half an hour depending on my mental state or the weather or any number of environmental factors. My mind has a tendency to wander and for some reason it likes the closet. I'll pick up a T-shirt and then a thought will come rushing in and I am lost. Today is a good day, as the meandering path of contemplation is not too terribly winding. . . .]

8:44 A.M. — *THE IMPORTANCE OF ACCESSORIZING*

[Shoes became an addiction for me about four years ago. I had worn the same pair of light-brown La Sportiva hiking boots every day forever when I tried on a pair of Puma tennis shoes. They were bright orange and I suspected they must require batteries to project such color, but they did not. I stared at my feet. I was mesmerized. These shoes have become like a drug and I now own them in every color of the visible spectrum. I choose the color for the day and locate a belt and a watch to set them off. . . .]

8:47 A.M. — *THE COVERING UP OF THINGS*

[I dress. . . .]

8:49 A.M. — *THE WONDER OF HAIR*

[I am back in the bathroom. I style my hair. . . .]

8:54 A.M. — *THE RIDICULOUS ROUTINE OF MAKING A BED*

[I relocate the alarm clock to its table and begin to make the bed. (Now, a small number of you reading this might be experiencing disappointment in having hoped for a more lengthy explanation of the happenings from 8:49–8:54, but alas that would be a book unto itself. For those of you who just skimmed right past the mention of hair with no curious wonderment, I would refer you to the author photo. As you can readily see, this is science. It indeed is a span of only five minutes, but what happens during that short period of time emerges at such a lightning pace, which would require such extremely intricate, micro-detailed descriptions that we are simply unable to explore it within the pages of this book. It is beyond the scope of our endeavor to contain such science here.) . . .]

9:00 A.M. — THE KISS

[I apologize for the graphic nature of this book. . . . I kiss my wife, Toni, and ask, "Chocolate or glazed?" then head for the door . . . uhhh . . . where are the . . . ?]

9:10 A.M. — THE RIDICULOUS ROUTINE OF SEARCHING FOR KEYS

[This happens every time I go anywhere. I am, at this point in my life, at a loss for how to fix the problem. . . . Okay, now with keys in hand I head for the door. . . .]

9:12 A.M. — THE IMPORTANCE OF THE CHOOSING OF MUSIC

[This will set the tone for the day. Your day must have an appropriate thematic background against which to unfold. I plug in my iPod. Today is Willie Nelson's. . . .]

9:15 A.M. — THE NECESSITY OF DONUTS

[I pull into Shipley Do-Nuts. I approach the counter. Crap. It's the chick who doesn't listen to me.

I recite, "Two plain cake, two regular chocolate covered, one large Dr Pepper, and one large decaf coffee—black." Doesn't listen.

"Okay." She retrieves the two cake donuts. "Two cake and what else for you?"

I recite, "Uh, and two regular chocolate covered and one

large Dr Pepper and one large decaf coffee—black—as I mentioned earlier."

"Okay." She retrieves the two regular chocolate covered donuts. "Two chocolate covered and what else for you?"

"Uh, one large Dr Pepper and one large decaf coffee—black—as also mentioned earlier."

"Okay. Anything else?"

"Yes. One large decaf coffee—black—as previously requested."

"Cream or sugar?" . . .]

9:21 A.M. — THE BALM OF WILLIE-AD

[I am back in my vehicle. Willie sings, "For all the girls I've loved before." I smile at the pleasure of my earlier thematic, musical-backdrop selection. Willie feels the pain and speaks with words and sounds I have only come across in dreams. I turn it up.]

And so the day continues in such a manner.

Where were the God moments? Where was Living Praise? Did praise happen? Could praise happen? What if it did? Were opportunities missed? Was praise just beneath the surface? Could it be a flood? Maybe it's just dammed? Maybe if the dam burst we would drown in it. Do we dare pick up a sledgehammer and start swinging? It could be difficult. It could wear at you. This could be hard labor. I don't know if I have the back for it. And I think I like my water in smaller doses. I like the sound of the drip. But there is cracking in my lips and they bleed when I smile. My hands are dry to the touch. So dry I can't feel you anymore. Pick it up? It is needed? It is what is necessary? I want to drown. I want a different air than what I've been breathing. I will swing. I will swing with all my might. I will swing until there is the sound of breaking. I will swing. Over and Over and Over and Over and Over and Over and Over and Over and Over and Over . . .

PRAISE

Becoming Who We Are (Part 1)

Praise is the culmination of our enjoyment of anything.

— C. S. Lewis

We naturally understand praise. As kids, we talk about our favorite toys; later we praise pizza and football players. Kids just know how to enjoy things. They give themselves fully to whatever has a hold on them. Remember as children how we would fearlessly hold up our favorite toy and petition anyone who was in close proximity to behold it?

"Look, Mom, look!"

We instinctively knew what it was to praise something. It's always been in us. We were created for it. It's a part of who we are. As kids, we were fabulous at it. But as adults we become self-conscious and awkward. Something gets lost. I think we do it to each other. At some point, I hold the toy up exultantly and you comment that it looks ridiculous to hold the toy up in such a way. It's not a cool toy like I believed it to be. It is worn and tired, you point out. And we slowly chip away at each other's protective coatings of innocence until one day we wake up and notice we are naked and people are pointing.

Occasionally, I'm watching a movie or reading words in a book or I'm walking down a street in California and the breeze on my skin feels full of water, like my arms are floating in a pool, and I'm inspired to live anew in an innocent rediscovering way I haven't thought of in a long time. Then just as I lean in to take a bite, to suck with all my might at the marrow, to breathe in with as much ferocity as I can muster, I see your eyes and hear your whispers.

"That's not polite. Use your silverware. If you don't have any we'll get you some. Please, we beg you. It is barbaric and difficult to watch. We have moved beyond this. Come with us. Please. We are becoming uncomfortable."

The moment I see a hill painted in greenest of grass, with long infinite blades waltzing in the wind, and make up my mind to sprint to the top, to give myself to gravity and let it roll me down, I hear "Dork!" shouted from behind me somewhere and I stop.

"What would they think? This is the thing of children. This is not civilized. Act your age."

This is what we have done to one another.

When was the last time you played with your food? I used to blow bubbles in my chocolate milk and nibble my Kraft American cheese singles into the shape of Texas.

I don't anymore.

LOOK ME IN THE EYE

I helped start a church in 1995 and I am still on staff there. My official title is Pastor of Music and Arts, which is meant to sound impressive and demanding of attention. You might think me above the effects of this "chipping at innocence" nonsense, untouched and unmarred, high in my ministerial spire. And you'd especially think me less conscious of self than most, with this appearance of bravery putting ink to paper for public consumption in book form. But it is untrue. The fact is I'm writing this while sitting safely at a table not looking at you. Our eyes have no chance of meeting for me to see your disapproval. I tend to have a difficult time with the whole eye-contact thing. I close my eyes when I sing. Not because I feel it, like the really good singers do, but because I can't bear your censorious stare.

I refer you again to the author photo. In typical picture-taking style, the photographer said, "One, two, three . . . ," then pushed the button, but two whole numbers is entirely too long to think about all the unfortunate people I would be making eye contact with, and I found that very disturbing, supposing it might be folks like yourself. Confident. Direct. People with social skills far exceeding mine. What choice did I have but to look away? I am sorry but I saw no other options. The photographer was quite impatient with me and showed frustration when my eyes drifted. He said things like,

"What is wrong with you?"

. . . and . . .

"Just keep looking at the camera please, until I say otherwise."

. . . mixed with seemly rhetorical questions like . . .

"Can you do that? Huh?"

Then I cracked and in blistering metaphor retorted:

"Thanks. Now I can't even find the courage to look at anything but the ground. It will be weeks before I'll again see the sky, and the sky has been so beautiful. Would you rob me of this? You people never think of the damage you inflict. Well, it's as devastating as a superimposed Godzilla. Am I to be your Tokyo? What harm have I brought to you? I didn't even look your direction and here you are stomping and blowing your fire about. There was supposed to be distance. Unspoken rules that prevented such things, and you deny them.

Are you the only one or will there be more who lumber into my hidden passageways hoping to set me straight, only to leave me in ruin because they don't know the weight of their breath? There is fire in their belly and I am fragile, and to breathe in this direction . . . "

Okay, I didn't say any of that but I thought it. Later. My point is we are all fragile. Somewhere along the way we abandoned abandon. Or perhaps we gained things that need to be discarded. We have covered ourselves. Someone pointed out that we were naked, and the clothing we have woven is bulky and pretentious. It hinders our freedom of movement. Expression with childlike spontaneity has become difficult. It bares too much of us.

Think back. Try hard to recall what praise in its undiluted purity felt like. When you would dance with your arms fully extended rather than elbows bent, folded closely to your person in such a guarded fashion. Remember how effortlessly we sang the praises of things we enjoyed? It was so easy and fluid and natural. What if this kind of praise freely leaked from us in delightful response to God? What if life were like that all the time? What if we were so moved by who God is, what He's done, what He will do, that praise, adoration, worship, whatever, continuously careened in our heads and pounded in our souls? What if praise were on the tip of our tongues like we were a loaded weapon in the hands of a trigger-happy meth addict and every moment might just set us off? This is what we will do for eternity. What makes us think our time on earth should be any different? What keeps it from being so?

HABIT

Becoming Who We Are (Part 2)

Spent needles, cigarette butts, spitting bits of fingernail, toilet seats in the upright position . . . For some reason, when I hear the word *habit* my head naturally inserts *bad* in front of it. Don't think ill of me, please. In my defense, I just took a quick survey of those sitting within the proximity of my voice in Barnes & Noble and four out of five said "bad" when I asked what they thought of when they heard the word *habit*. I feel better. So . . . I hear *habit* and I think of things we human beings do that I perceive are not particularly positive. According to my thoroughly unscientific bookstore survey, odds are you do, too. Habits like drinking milk from the carton, cussing, buying Top 40 music, killing things, grinding teeth, clicking a pen over and over and over, cleaning ears with sharp instruments like, say, keys or a light saber, burning things that look flammable, sleeping while driving. It's incredible the things that become habitual.

I sucked my thumb as a kid, long after I became aware that it was embarrassing to do so. I had been told and told to refrain, and I did not. I had been told it would give me buckteeth, but I sucked on. One morning a trip to the pharmacy commenced for the purchase of a horribly bitter liquid that had the appearance of clear fingernail polish but whose sadistic hidden intent was to break strong-willed kids of their thumb-sucking habits. My mom gave me money and waited in the car as I completed the transaction with our family pharmacist friend. The objective here was trauma. You don't give a kindergartener cash money and send them wandering into a pharmacy unless you are hoping to make a durable impression. I couldn't see over the counter. I just said my name and handed the guy in white the pretty green paper with the strange smell. He handed me a bag full of fright. That night my parents and I ceremoniously applied the liquid to both thumbnails. In a matter of days I had developed a small amount of love for this liquid. Sure it was acidicly pungent and I'm certain it would overpower weaker children and bring them to submission but I . . . I would not bend. I would suck my thumb and grow buckteeth.

THAT THING YOU DO

A habit is an act acquired by experience and performed regularly and automatically. A habit is influenced not only by elements that bring the behavior about but also by rewards or punishments that follow the behavior. Self-destructive habits can be eliminated by behavior modification or counterconditioning techniques. These involve increasing one's awareness of the act, interrupting its performance so that it no longer seems such a natural thing to do, and reinforcing another act as a competitor.[2] Habits involve no conscious choice among alternatives.

TWENTY-ONE DAYS

Years ago a friend told me that an action repeated for a minimum of twenty-one days is likely to become a permanent habit. So I thought I'd give it a shot. I would choose a habit that was nonsensical but not too nonsensical. After much thought I decided that my trained response to "Hello" or "How's it going?" or "Hi" would be to salute and wink. In the beginning it was quite fun. Some pal would walk in a room and say, "What's up?" and I would raise hand over eye in quick, sharp movements and wink while responding, "Not much." *It was beauty. The internal joy this brought was overwhelming.* It was the perfect habit to form. It was quirky but legitimate. Impossible to tell if I was serious or not. I could be. I mean, if you hadn't known me you might not even notice that I'd just saluted you and winked as we passed in the hall. But it really looked absurd. The "Sunshine Sailor" is what I called it.

Sometimes I would forget. My pal would walk in and say, "What's up?" and I'd naturally say, "Hey," without even looking up. Then moments later it would dawn on me I had neglected the salute. Immediately, and regardless of changes to the original environment, I would rise to my feet, throw hand to forehead in exaggerated gesture, deliver a brawny "Hello," and wink. This was my counterconditioning technique, and it could get a small bit embarrassing. I appeared insane. You did not want to do the Sunshine Sailor after the fact. I soon wanted to keep these time-delayed occurrences to a minimum. Sure enough, before long I didn't even think about it. The Sunshine Sailor had become my salutation—until one day when I saluted the convenience store clerk and realized it did nothing inside. There was no suppressed smile. There was no choked-back laughter. Nothing joyous bursting in my chest. There should have been celebration in the knowledge that it had worked. It was habit. I had done it. Instead, that day became for me the first of twenty-one attempts to sever the Sunshine Sailor from my person.

THE GOOD, THE BAD, AND . . .

It seems for most bad habits we display, there was never any intentional formation. Most alcoholics do not sit down and think, "Okay, just twenty-one days and I'll need this stuff like water." Most nail biters do not think, "I love the taste of my fingernails and the feeling of tearing them down to the quick. I really need to consider doing it more often." No, usually destructive habits are formed more subtly with very little thought and planning.

Good habits seem more difficult to manage. Maybe it's just me, but things like brushing your teeth, exercising, proper eating, saying "yes, sir" and "no, sir," and sending Mother's Day flowers seem much harder to acquire than, say, burping at the table. Why does it seem like the formation must be much more intentional in our adoption of good habits?

I'm convinced it's because we are bent, deficient, broken. Things aren't right. Things aren't as they were intended. Things aren't as they were at the start. Innocence is gone, and left alone in our depraved state we tend to choose destructive paths. Oh, we have choice. We have will, this capacity to choose among alternative courses of action and to act on the choice made.[3] But good habits seem counterintuitive. When we do find the will and courage to head down that narrow path, we often find that even then we still have a deep capacity for taking beautiful things and turning them into hideous remnants of what was intended.

For instance, we want to exercise more or eat healthier, so we set out to develop routines that help us accomplish this. Then one day we find ourselves standing in front of a mirror, flexing, and realize we've been doing this for the last thirty minutes. It dawns on us that we've become complete narcissists. Okay. Sorry. Bad example. That's never happened to me, either. I actually avoid mirrors for the most part and have only flexed on three occasions in my life, all occurring before the age of ten. Let me try again. Countless times I have tried to develop a habit of having a "quiet time." Sometimes it would stick. Sometimes it would not. Guilt would be thick when it would not. But for a long period it became what I did first thing every day. *It was beauty. The internal joy it brought was overwhelming.* Then at some point it went hollow. It's not that it was a bad idea to form a habit of a quiet time, but the habit had slyly begun to suck the life out of my relationship with God. I had fallen in love with my spirituality rather than with the one whom I sought, and in the end it left me void and wanting.

A frightening aspect of habit attached to our spiritual formation is that inherent in the idea of habit is the possibility for meaningless ritual. With the formation of habit there is a subtle abdication of consciousness in our actions. This can twist things that were intended to bring life into cold and empty ritualistic experiences. Indeed we are broken. We do bad things without thinking and when we try to do good things they often end up warped. How can we maintain life in our spiritual formation?

NATURAL VERSUS FORMED

It might be helpful for us to first make a couple of subtle shifts in our understanding of habit. Instead of describing habits in terms of good and bad, let's talk in terms of natural versus formed habits. Eating. Breathing. Your heartbeat. No one ever told you to do any of these things. You were made for this. They came naturally. They did not come awkwardly with repeated failures and the deep need of positive and negative reinforcement such as when you decided to form the ability of chopstick usage. There was no inelegant fumbling as with the sticks. True, you can now deliver tiny grains of rice to the wanting cavity in your face with little thought but it did not come without bits of rice in your lap and cramps in the tender palm of your hand.

THE BREATHING IN AND OUT AND IN. . .

You came from the embryonic fluid, and there was a need for air in your lungs. A wanting for O_2 in your veins. And so you exhaled liquid, gave a few coughs, and breathed in. This holy ritual of breathing began. It is necessary for living. I have tried to neglect it from time to time and it just never works out for very long. Once it was a large piece of hamburger that was causation, but for the most part it was always consciously agreed upon that I'd like to do without breathing for a bit. Usually this had to do with being beneath the surface of water, but there were other times—such as in boring classes in high school with large clocks on the wall, whose beckoning second hands left me no choice, or numbing Sunday-night sermons that prompted my Timex Ironman to call from my wrist in challenging tone—that found me engrossed in oxygen deprivation for sport. Testing your red blood cell count can be fun *and* pass the time in an agreeable manner.

There is a tunnel on I-70 about sixty miles west of Denver. It is called the Eisenhower Memorial Tunnel. The westbound tunnel is 1.693 miles long. Every time I drive through it I hold my breath because I heard that it is lucky to do so when driving through tunnels. I don't really believe it will bring me luck, but it seems a worthy challenge and I enjoy a challenge. 1.693 miles at 60 miles an hour = 1 minute and 41.58 seconds lacking oxygen. I've only made it all the way through on four occasions. Three of them I was driving. This is not recommended, as one of the side effects of not breathing is light-headedness, and this does not mingle well with the operation of vehicles or heavy machinery.

For the most part, successful oxygen-less tunnel passage depends upon driving conditions and traffic flow. Tenacious mental focus is fundamental—absolute mind-over-body control. I will grace you with a brief glimpse into the psychological tenacity that is necessary to accomplish such a feat. What follows would be my typical cerebral process during passage. Please hold your breath while reading:

- *Upon entering tunnel*—"Okay, deep breath . . . "
- *1/4 of the way through*—"This is easy. My lungs are huge. I am the greatest breath holder ever."
- *1/2 way through*—"Freaking Taurus! What the fat are you thinking?! You can't be in the *passing* lane not passing! Do not do this. MOVE! MOVE!"
- *3/4 of the way through*—"Just concentrate on tapping your foot. No, bite your lip. No, listen to this song. I'm so not going to make it. Fake breathe. Yeah. Just move your *stomach* in and out and your body will think you're working on the problem it senses and it will relax a bit, therefore buying more time. I'm so not going to make it."
- *Almost there*—"I can't believe it! There it is! Now I understand what they mean, the light at the end of the tunnel. They're right. It's beautiful! It's freeing! I will make it. This is something to be proud of. I can do without things others need. My tolerance for discomfort could crush those who would question. What? . . . NO! . . . TAURUS, YOU DID NOT JUST MAKE AN UNSIGNALED LANE CHANGE AND STOP IN THE MIDDLE OF THE INTERSTATE!"

Air comes flooding in and it is the most amazing thing. My capacity for missing something is much deeper than I realize.

THE BEATING IN YOUR CHEST

And there is heartbeat. It is electricity keeping our sinus rhythm. Electricity! Why it's not some other power, like fusion on a subatomic level or squirrels on treadmills, I don't know, but it is not—we are electric. There is lighting in our cells. There is rhythm in our nerves. Firings happen and the heart contracts and the blood goes from here to there, and mine is somehow not right. Extra bursts in the Bundle of His.[4]

Last September there was an irregular tapping in my chest. A tapping on my breastplate from the inside. Not a gentle, constant drum but an erratic thud pounding at volatile intervals. The tapping would be slow and with the velocity of the index finger and then WHAM! a fist coming through. There would be racing and silence. It was maddening. My wife took me to the ER. I am afraid of doctors. I am afraid of dentists. Anything medical. Anyone in white. Anyone with access to needles and the education to use them. I can't look at needles without feeling faint. I've never actually fainted, but I'm certain that this is that feeling. The kind lady in green hooks me up to wires. She studies the sheet of paper. She then asks me, "Are you on any street drugs?"

"Excuse me?"

"Are you on any street drugs?"

I laugh nervously, "Uh, I'm not sure what you mean, but I don't think so. What do you mean 'street drugs'? Like drugs from the street? Like not Tylenol? No, I'm not on street drugs, I'm certain. Yes, I've thought about it, and no, I am not on street drugs."

She doesn't believe me. (See author photo.) She says there will be tests and that I should just tell her now. It will make things go more quickly.

"I swear I'm not on street drugs. I don't even know what those are! You mean like crack or something?"

She goes to get a needle and a specimen cup.

I don't really like specimen cups, either. My first specimen cup was given to me in elementary school during PE class by a large black lady dressed in white. She handed me the small plastic receptacle and told me to go pee in it. I made my way alone to the bathroom with only the cup as companion and did what she asked. But it turns out there was more pee in my seven-year-old bladder than would fit in such a tiny cup. She hadn't made mention of what I was to do with all the excess, so it went everywhere. All over my hands and shoes and pants. I was embarrassed and confused, but I faithfully topped it off with satisfaction and pride, then I delicately carried the overflowing cup of gold back with all the coordination of a second-grader. Unfortunately, the kind black lady in white seemed neither moderately impressed by my efforts nor as interested as I in the surface tension of urine as she sang at me, "Ooooo, go dump some of that out, sugar!"

And now here I was again in a bathroom holding the same tiny cup, recalling all of this. I was amazed at how I still could feel the embarrassment. For a moment I thought the whole thing might be fun to reenact. That would teach the lady in green. She was probably expecting it anyway with all the street drugs coursing through my veins. But I did not.

After much prodding and poking and X-rays and more needles and an IV, it was eventually explained to me that I had Lone (Idiopathic) Atrial Fibrillation: A-Fib without any accompanying or triggering heart disease or other illness. I have since met many others who have experienced the same troubling tapping as I did that September 16th. I've a few friends who are on anti-arrhythmic medications and one who insists on troubling me with stories of his focal catheter ablation (pulmonary vein ablation).

At 7:00 p.m. I was given a drug intravenously that would convert my electrical pulses back to normal. I watched as the line on the heart monitor, which had been nothing but erratic scribbles, turned into equally spaced outlined peaks of green. It was amazing watching it happen on the screen, but the feeling in my chest is unforgettable. I'd already forgotten what a correct beating in the chest felt like. When things went right, there was this calm. It was as if calm had been an abstraction until then, an idea I'd never really grasped. The difference between arrhythmia and sinus rhythm was more vast than can be described. It was the difference between a rock skipping across choppy water and one sinking fluidly toward the sandy bottom. The difference between a jackhammer and a feather. Between movement and stasis. Between a bomb and a kiss. And the difference made all the difference. There are nights I lie awake with my hand on my chest wondering if the tapping will start.

TAKE ME BACK TO THE START

Things are often more meaningful when they come out of natural need. You don't think about the beating of your heart until things go amiss. And there aren't many things much sweeter than breath after the lack of it. Food tastes better when you're hungry, not just because your watch says twelve o'clock. And sleep! What if you could just take a nap whenever you felt tired? And how calamitous when these things aren't happening when required? We were made to eat. We were made to breathe. This is the kind of ritual we are seeking. The one that is as natural as the beating in our chest, the one that is in us from the beginning, the one that without, we cease to truly live. The one that, once we put our finger on it, is as routine and life-giving as our pulse.

This thing that was intended from the start has become buried, and once uncovered it comes bursting as if through a mountain of dirt and rock from the end of a tunnel with bad florescent lighting and traffic into sunshine and blue sky. This is the habit I'm interested in rediscovering. It is the deep breath after having forgotten to breathe. The one we were made for. Remember the start? Our beginnings? In the beginning there was the recognition that the source of all things was Creator God. There was relational communion with our Maker in all that was life, and we were alive, really alive. He was in the breeze and under rocks and in our love and in our skin and in His voice, oh, His voice. There was no knowledge of anything but what was good, and gratefulness beat in our bones. This is the kind of praise that is sweeter and stronger than anything conjured up in an order of worship on Sunday or during our scheduled morning quiet time or in the songs of the "contemporary worship" service Saturday evening or in classrooms of scholarly study.

PRAISE HABIT

Becoming Who We Are (Part 3)

My intent here is not to tear away at spiritual disciplines or discard them as dated contrivances but to inject some portion of freedom and life into them. It is my belief that we were made to praise and that the original intentions for it might have been bigger and sweeter than most of us have dreamed or that a scheduled moment could properly contain. We find ourselves in a dynamic, fluid relationship with the divine, where there is such a perpetual movement and flow that a static, formulaic approach undermines and lessens what could exist. It is hamburger stuck in our esophagus. We were meant for every moment to be fully alive with this dynamic relating and vibrant presence of hope in finding our Maker near us. Again, nothing is nonspiritual. Grasping this does not diminish the necessity of our disciplines; it only brings to them more depth and beauty.

In the article "Fly on the Wall," Dallas Willard, Larry Crabb, and John Ortberg are talking through how spiritual formation actually happens. At some point they start discussing the importance of putting Scripture into plain language. Ortberg starts quoting from Willard's book *The Divine Conspiracy*, where Willard unpacks "kingdom of heaven." Midway through the conversation, Ortberg says:

> But to think about the use of "heavens" in Scripture as the sphere in which God is present, which means right here. So to look at the prayer as saying, "My father (who loves me intently and has my best interests at heart) is all around me. My Father, who is closer than the air I breathe." And then that becomes a thought.
>
> There is something about thoughts to me where they get stale.

DW: They get very stale.

LC: New language helps, personal vernacular.

JO: Yep, just the right word to take something familiar like, "Our Father who art in heaven," and say, "Our Father who is closer than the air I breathe." My mind can run with that a little bit. And eventually that gets stale, and I have to keep thinking things out over and over. But it helps. The process of putting it in new words never gets done.[5]

I think this is true of our disciplines as well. Remember the Sunshine Sailor? There's a cycle that takes place where we find/experience a spiritual habit that brings connection and meaning, but eventually even that thing will get stale and something else will need to find its way in. We need to continually redefine what our spiritual disciplines look like, an importunate redefining of the habits that define us. There is inherent danger in ritual, but there is still the necessity in our movement toward Christ and His intentions for our lives. There is the definitive need for a continual shedding of depravity and the taking on of His righteousness. There is the need for us to embrace this new way of living that is found in the person of Christ. Or perhaps it's more than that: allowing His life to engulf and cover us. We must continually seek ways to place ourselves in this embrace.

The spiritual life is first of all a life. It is not merely something to be known and studied, it is to be lived.
— THOMAS MERTON, *THOUGHTS IN SOLITUDE*

There is risk in placing yourself in the way of His embrace. Richard Foster speaks of spiritual disciplines in the illustrative terms of a path on a trepidatious ledge set between two sheer drop-offs. On one side is the danger of a works-based legalism and on the other an abyss of a faith devoid of action.[6] But the path is life; it is real living.

So here is the process I propose for putting our understanding of habit in terms of the spiritual formation of praise into new words:

What if we added another definition of habit to our ideas of natural versus formed that might move us beyond our sterile idea of ritual or our paralyzed state of legalistic fear and help us rediscover what was meant to be second nature? I dug around a little and found that the word *habit* has its roots in Middle English, "clothing," Old French, "clothing, behavior custom," and ultimately, in the Latin word *habitus,* which means "condition, character" and *habere,* meaning "to have, to hold." With a tad more linguistic study I discovered that at one point in history, habit became particularly associated with a distinctive dress or costume, especially of a religious order.[7] This I liked. As soon as I read that definition, a memory of Audrey Hepburn in the movie *The Nun's Story* came quickly in, flooding thought.

My wife loves old movies. Watches them constantly. Jumpy black-and-white pictures with bad monophonic sound and she is lost. I have the decidedly supreme privilege of watching quite a number of them myself because I like to be near her, and to be near her means watching much of old Hollywood as it flickers in our TV room. There are a few old movie stars that I fancy, and Audrey Hepburn is one of them. She is completely adorable in a cleverly delicate, tiny mouse sort of way. And she has style. She's known for it—a quintessential style icon. She was the birth of "the little black dress." For years, designers have mimicked her fashion from movies like *Breakfast at Tiffany's*[8] and *Funny Face* and *Roman Holiday* and *Sabrina.*

However, in the 1959 movie *The Nun's Story,* Audrey was not dressed so fashionably chic as was her big-screen custom. No, in this cinematic feature she donned the habit of a religious sister. Due to the universality of the Catholic Church, when we hear the word *nun,* images of starched linen headbands and wimples, long heavy dresses, and gracefully dripping black veils come to mind. Granted, for some this image represents a dated way of living for the fashionable nun on the go, but for many this characteristic black-and-white dress is a symbol of holiness—a redolent icon that has been a definitive portrait of the Catholic Church for nearly two thousand years. A few of you might have also found thoughts of the Nunzilla wind-up toy (appendix C) or the ever popular Fighting Nun puppet dancing in your head, but the reason those are so humorous is due to the cultural stigma that nuns have within our society. Their way of life is so mysterious and *other-than* the typical Western consumerist experience. To see a nun in full habit is so visually compelling, I am usually stopped in my tracks and found lingering to watch their movements and interactions.

One particularly searing encounter innocuously occurred in Times Square, NYC. Amid the bright lights and store windows satiated with color, there they were, impossible to miss, in glorious black and white. Two women lost in conversation. It is a most haunting thing to observe such visual contrasts unfurl in front of you. The habit demands attention and will not let go. What is this life they have chosen? How do you put that thing on? What is a wimple anyway?

In *The Nun's Story* there is a scene where Audrey Hepburn's character participates in the clothing ceremony that was once common for all sisters entering the devout life. During the ceremony, the sister would receive her consecrated garb and new religious name. She would then lie flat on the ground before the altar as a black funeral pall was placed over her and candles burned at each corner of her body. The choir would sing a sequence from a requiem Mass, symbolizing her death to self. Her old life was gone. What was before this moment had vanished. A new name, a new set of clothes, and a new way of living had begun.

By the tenth century, the ceremony closely resembled an elaborate "secular" marriage service with a silver ring placed on the nun's finger and her recitation of, "I am espoused to Him Whom angels serve; whose beauty sun and moon behold with wonder."[9]

In her book *The Habit: A History of the Clothing of Catholic Nuns*, Elizabeth Kuhns writes:

> For these nuns, the habit is a wearable sacramental with a supernatural character that cannot be replicated in secular clothing. . . . It is important to remember that clothing is a uniquely human characteristic, a silent but powerful medium from which we can learn who we are and what we value. Clothing defines gender, status, beauty, and ideology, and it can be found in virtually every culture. It touches on human history, psychology, sociology, economics, aesthetics, technology, customs, laws, attitudes and values. . . . The habit has the glamour of fashion while being antifashion. . . . The sighting of a nun in habit remains for most of us a notable event, because what the habit proclaims is something so counterculture and so radical, we cannot help but to react with awe and reverence or with suspicion and disdain.[10]

This is the kind of Praise Habit I wish to pursue. It is the one we already have on, the one we find ourselves in.

In our encounter with Christ we, too, have been laid down, devastated by His grace. We have been covered by this same grace. We have been taken from death to life by this grace. Our identity is changed. What was before this new beginning has vanished. We have been given new clothes. We have put on Christ. We are found dressed in His rescue, redemption, and righteousness and, aware of this rescue, we spew forth praise. We wear this very rescue into our relationships, into our interactions with pals and family and work and play. It is present in our embodiments or neglections of justice, in our contention or ignore-ance of the poor, of the widows, of the sick, of those in need. To wear the rescue of Christ into every moment is for every moment to become alive with the possibility of revelation. With the awareness of rescue, things unsuspected will begin to revelate redemption.

What choice is there but to respond in praise? Praise is fundamentally a responding to the initiations and intimations of God. The way of *living praise* sets out to find God's revelation, to carry God's intentions for His creation into our everyday comings and goings. And this way of life should be so compelling and mysterious and other-than that people see us coming from a long way off and it stops them in their tracks and they wait and watch just to see our exchanges and wonder at this life that has been chosen and how to put it on and what is this deeper, truer way of living anyway?

A nun does not get up each morning and go to the closet and think to herself, *Hmmm. I wonder what to wear today.* The habit *is* what she wears. It is what covers her. It is what identifies her. Our condition is the same. Our habit is the Christ. He is what covers us. He is what identifies us. We wear Him into every moment, and when we live with this awareness, we *PRAISE CHRIST* (appendix A).

THE PSALMS

Living Praise

Did you see that? It was like the moment in the Shell Game involving that subtle slight of hand where the pea goes from here to there with such speed and stealth that it's almost invisible. What tricky wordplay I have concocted. With deft illusion I have instantaneously transformed *Praise Habit* into *Praise Christ*. It is a rabbit pulled quickly from a hat. It is the card you were thinking of. It is the nickel pulled from your ear. Here's what happened. I'll slow it down for you. Okay, so if our "Habit" is Christ, if He is what covers us, if He is our garment, then with that small amount of wordplay we replace the word *Habit* with our newly, more specifically defined *Christ,* suddenly *Praise Habit* becomes *Praise Christ.* Can you feel what that means? We become the living praise that we are. It is a shifting of realities. To be fully present in the rescue and re-creation of Christ is to embrace what God does for us, and this is the best thing we can do for Him.[11]

For most of us this natural ritual of praise, this offering of our everyday ordinary life, this new reality of identity, is as foreign as crop dusting or macromolecular biophysics. We have forgotten. We have held our breath too long. Our rhythm is thrown off. There are extra firings; nerve endings have grown that set our hearts beating after other stuff. Lesser things that captured our affections have displaced the reality of the centrality of God. And we lie in our beds at night with our hands on our chests.

This is disheartening in that we know our living could be deeper and we have settled, and even more so in that our Praise Habit has potential to be missional in its very living. Missional is apparently not common to contemporary language, as Microsoft Word's Spell Check is currently alerting me it doesn't exist. What I mean is that our *HABIT of PRAISE*, in its unpolluted state, is attractive and fashionable in its antifashion. Much of our energy as Christians-attempting-to-live-devoted-lives centers on the development of patterns or activities to strengthen or deepen our "spiritual" selves, things previously mentioned, such as corporate worship, or scholastic theological study, or quiet times, or praying before meals. And we think that if we pray before a meal, it will set this moment apart and other unbelieving peoples might observe our devoutness and we will make a statement that will surely cause them to stop in their tracks. Then leaving that brief holy event well behind, feeling our obligation to "otherness" consummated, we engross ourselves in the devouring of burgers and French fries. But it is in the moments that follow our prayers that we are able to follow the trail of our true affections, our hidden motivations. It is in the gluttonous idolatry or tearful gratefulness that we consume the burger. It is in our conversations over the meal—the valuing or devaluing of the ones with whom we find ourselves exchanging conversation. It is found in the gratuity at the end of the meal. While somebody else is talking, I usually find myself busily plotting ways to divert the subject matter back to myself rather than lending heart and ear and thought to their discourse.

It is indeed a sad thing to discover we have been functioning in unintended and unredeemed ways, performing rituals of shiny, sequined adulation that we put on with good intention. We saw a brightly colored sweater and thought, *It is fall and the leaves are turning and this will bring comfort*, so we pull it on over our habit, over our Christ. It feels big and bulky, but people have told us it looks good on us. It makes us look thinner. It brings out our eyes. But we've looked in the mirror and have seen our eyes. They look hollow and tired. There is an absence of life. We know because we've felt things in our chest go right at one time. We know because we've, on occasion, seen fiery love staring back at us from the mirror.

Sometimes it takes staring into the mirror first thing every morning before we notice all the layers we are wearing. Other times it takes only a chance glance in a store window as we walk down the street, briefly catching our reflection. Most times we turn and continue on our way, resolutely refusing to peer into the next shop glass, telling ourselves that what we observed in reflection was quite becoming. But occasionally we find the courage to stand in that revealing moment and slowly peel everything off until we can clearly see again our Christ that defines and identifies us. And we walk away, leaving everything else behind—the colorful sweaters and hoodies and button-up Polos and vintage T-shirts that we paid too much for and the argyle socks and the deck shoes and the blue-jean jacket and the parachute pants (some of this stuff we've worn way too long) and the bib to prevent us from getting anything on us and the brand-new Von Dutch lid of corduroy. We turn and walk away from these shed layers and then sadly, thirty-four steps later, we stare past our reflection in the next shop window at the coolly dressed mannequin and we go inside. . . .

How can we continually rid ourselves of these bulky, pretentious clothes and become who we are underneath it all? What would it look like to wear the identity of Christ in a way that defines us and our moments? And what would it look like to carry rescue into every moment?

I think the Psalms can help us exhale what has been causing our labored breath or perhaps be just the mirror we've needed to walk past in order to catch a glimpse of how truly cumbersome these extra layers really are.

The Psalms are a literature of dialogue. They are a script of relationship, a two-sided, genuine conversation. A picture of revealing and response. They capture the experience of life as a child of God. The reason they do this so well is because they are not censored or clean. They articulate horrific loss and anger as well as they do celebration and joy. There is room and necessity for both in this conversation. Walter Brueggemann, in *The Message of the Psalms*, says:

Much Christian piety and spirituality is romantic and unreal in its positiveness. As children of the Enlightenment, we have censored and selected around the voice of darkness and disorientation, seeking to go from strength to strength, from victory to victory. But such a way not only ignores the Psalms; it is a lie in terms of our experience. . . . The Jewish reality of exile, the Christian confession of crucifixion and cross, the honest recognition that there is an untamed darkness in our life that must be embraced—all of that is fundamental to the gift of new life.[12]

Our lives are not painted in so positive a light as much of our traditions of piety might lead us to believe. There is a romantic tendency in our selections of liturgy to make use of only the careful and pleasant Psalms that in Brueggemann's words "support the polite hermeneutic of the church."[13] It is no wonder we have trouble when trying to fit our "spirituality" into all the stuff of life because we've neglected to bring all the stuff of life into our "spirituality." There is impoliteness in our experience of living. There is darkness and pain. But the wonder and the joy and the surprise are that even in the middle of darkness and loss is the unexpected presence of God.

Luther concluded that the Psalms apprehended the whole gospel of God. Calvin referred to the Psalms as an "anatomy of the soul," holding both the cost and the beauty of life with God. The Psalms are the prayers and songs of *real* people. They are the prayers and songs that erupt from *real* life. They do not hold the polished, sophisticated language you might expect.[14]

When we think of the Psalms, we often think of David, the most well-known author of these passages. David and all of his flawed and faultless brilliance are present here. David was a kid. David was a king. David was a fugitive on the run. David was an adulterer. David was a murderer. David was a liar. David was repentant. David was a lover of God. The best lover of God. David was an example of living praise. His praise was loud, soft, silent, active, latent, inappropriate, terrified, incarnate, communal, awe-filled, humble, undignified. Here is an example of becoming who you were meant to be. His awareness of rescue is deep and continual. The struggle is present and approachable in these songs with a glimpse at the potential brilliance of the intrusion of divine relationship into every encounter.

What follows are twenty-one psalms, with hope that they drift into your life in a way that rattles and changes—in a way that sneaks in and subverts your current living until you find yourself coming to life with vivacity and freedom of movement, with the sparkling, flammable words dancing in your soul, "I'm alive, I'm alive, I'm alive, I'm alive, I'm alive, I'm alive, I'm alive, I'm alive . . . ," until tears spill down in belief.

LECTIO DIVINA

Approaching the Psalms

I used a process of Scripture meditation known as *lectio divina* in my encounter with the following psalms. Simply described, it is a thoughtful, repeated reading and praying of the passage. (Appendix B gives a more detailed description of this meditation method.)

Read these psalms. As a phrase grabs you, ruminate on it. Turn it over in your heart. Let the Scriptures squeeze you. Then do as I. *Create.* Journal, paint, sculpt, sing, dance, write. Let your encounter cause something to spill out.

PSALM 1

How well God must like you —
    you don't hang out at Sin Saloon,
    you don't slink along Dead-End Road,
    you don't go to Smart-Mouth College.

Instead you thrill to GOD's Word,
    you chew on Scripture day and night.
    You're a tree replanted in Eden,
    bearing fresh fruit every month,
    Never dropping a leaf,
    always in blossom.

You're not at all like the wicked,
    who are mere windblown dust —
    Without defense in court,
    unfit company for innocent people.

    GOD charts the road you take.
    The road they take is Skid Row.

It is surely no accident that Psalm 1 is the first in this collection of prayers and songs. It gives argument for everything that follows. It sets the tone for the entire hymnic tradition for the people of Israel. It gives reason for their eruptions of chorus. It is a declaration of the intentions of obedience for their life of worship: "to order and conduct all of life in accordance with God's purpose and ordering of creation."[15] To obey the commands of God brings life. To ignore them brings death. In this psalm there is a vast distinction between those who live in ways that were intended from the start and those whose lives are distortions of God's dreams for humanity. God had given His people Torah, the Law, rules to live by, and you either embraced these words with the living of them or you rejected them with a life of disregard, and it is the difference between life and death.

To live how you were intended, to interact with God's creation in ways that were His breathings, brings life. Real life. Not just tedious existence, but life that breathes like a tree by a cool river with the grass of Eden stretching broad and embowering under limb. It is beauty. It is bending in the breeze, arms wide, leaves dancing. And to live in ways that twist and distort His creation brings death. Real death. Not just the redundant (none of us are getting out of here alive) burying of corpses, but the walking around kind that tastes of dust rather than the Maker's exhale of love. It is repulsive. It doesn't hold together. It is not the genesis-shape imagined for a human.

This is the argument proposed in the first psalm, that praise erupts from "right living." We usually miss the psalm's intent when we attempt to define right living. Our cultural conditioning of Western nationalistic Christianity typically sends us headlong into pharisaical discussions of R-rated movies and cussing and drinking and smoking and the dangers of associating with heathen who do any of the previously mentioned activities. I am familiar with a copious quantity of people who do *not* participate in any of these activities yet walk around lifeless, as dead and intriguing as a pile of dirt. The conversation is bigger and grander than this. Right living doesn't have its roots in conservative American politics; it is not simply adhering to conventional ideas of morality, propriety, or decorum. It is the living of Eden, it is living in the way that was intended, it is *true* living.

This mirror of the psalms and this argument for right living exposes our distortions right here at the start. We are a long way from "the beginning." It has been many days since we have felt the grass of Eden underfoot. But there is a right living that is ordered by the ways of Christ. There is a right living that erupts from the embrace of grace. This is the reason for the psalms, this is why there is cause for praise: we have a God who is bringing us back and we are responding with every heartbeat. There is a choosing. Life is not trivial—how it is lived is decisive.

# PSALM 8

God, brilliant Lord,
  yours is a household name.

Nursing infants gurgle choruses about you;
  toddlers shout the songs
  That drown out enemy talk,
  and silence atheist babble.

I look up at your macro-skies, dark and enormous,
  your handmade sky-jewelry,
  Moon and stars mounted in their settings.
  Then I look at my micro-self and wonder,
  Why do you bother with us?
  Why take a second look our way?

Yet we've so narrowly missed being gods,
  bright with Eden's dawn light.
  You put us in charge of your handcrafted world,
  repeated to us your Genesis-charge,
  Made us lords of sheep and cattle,
  even animals out in the wild,
  Birds flying and fish swimming,
  whales singing in the ocean deeps.

God, brilliant Lord,
  your name echoes around the world.

Star, star, teach me how to shine.

— THE FRAMES

We are smitten with fame. Can't take our eyes off it. Oh, some of us try to play it cool. I've met a few famous folks, and I cannot play it cool.

Once I was in the LA airport and saw Richard Simmons. *The* fitness icon Richard Simmons in all of his *Sweatin' to the Oldies* glory. White puffy gym socks, white Reebok high-tops, tiny red-and-white-striped jogging shorts, loosely fitted red tank top climaxing in his dandelion head of hair. I tried to play it cool. "Don't stare," I told myself. "Just look natural." I began a covert search of my bag for the camera. I tried desperately to appear unrattled, but his shoes—his shoes were so white! How could shoes be so white? And the socks, how could you find socks that puffy? Where do you *buy* socks like that? I had just begun replaying in my head the last time I had seen him on the *Late Show with David Letterman*—Mr. Letterman had sprayed him with a fire extinguisher and Richard had gotten really upset—when all of a sudden our eyes met. Yes, mine and Richard's! I was busted. He knew. I had tried to play it cool but now here I was, found out. Suddenly, Richard was running toward me, arms stretched, wing-like, equaled in width by his smile that was a flood spilling everywhere. At first, I froze. Then with no resolute thought I began to run toward him in a slow, undecided gait. My feet were lead and difficult to acquire full cooperation from. I slowed to a stop just in front of him, not sure what to do next, and then he hugged me. His dandelion head was pressed to my chest and his arms were coupled around me, and I think he was jumping a small bit. At some point I noticed that I was hugging him, too. I couldn't discern when that had happened, but apparently there was a conversation between my brain and muscle tissue, and synapses had fired, and here I was in the LAX in full embrace with *the fitness icon* Richard Simmons.

I just can't play it cool. No, if I'm in the same room and you are famous I will stare and ask for pictures and shake your hand and ask you dumb questions like, "So is it cold when you're sprayed with a fire extinguisher? I've always wondered 'cause fire is so hot and you know that stuff must be cold if it puts it out. You know?" And you will want me to go away but I will stay until you ask me to leave, nicely at first and then you will stop smiling. Your people will grab me under my arms, with fingers tightly around my biceps, and they will force distance between us and you will get on a plane and leave, and I will talk about meeting you the rest of the day or month or maybe in a book I will write because you are famous and it is worth the telling to anyone who will listen. It comes up all the time. Conversations about weather or donuts and somehow I will have worked in the story about meeting Richard. Or maybe I will tell you of Mel Gibson and the firmness of his handshake. Or I'll insist you hear about the time I bumped into Martin Short in a restroom and how he emptied all of his pockets on the counter. Or when I met Bob Dole in a Texas airport and how he didn't talk in third person one single time while kindly posing for a picture with me. How I told him I'd voted for him in his run for the White House and the strangeness of his response, "Well, we've got 'em outnumbered," and how confused I was and still am by that statement. Did he know he lost? Was he that much smarter and I just didn't understand? How these few spoken words keep me awake in bed some nights.

We are hooked on fame. There are magazines and websites and television shows that allow us—even encourage us—to peer into the lives of the famous. See what they eat, wear, date, think, believe, hope, drink, drive, and where we can spot them next, and if I meet them I will tell you.

I have a mildly famous friend who thinks himself an astronomer. At least, to hear him talk you'd think so. He has this book that he keeps beside his bed. It is filled with images of space. It has facts about galaxies and how big they are or how far away they are with this number of stars and that number of planets. He has a lot of it memorized and sounds really smart rattling things off like, "Hey, look at this one. This is a picture of spiral galaxy NGC-4414. It's around sixty million light years from here![16] Can you believe it?" He says that he has been reading this book as his devotional each morning. To resize him. He stares into the grandness of the cosmos to see the macro large big-time scale of things and, in comparison, his micro tiny-scale small-time fleeting moment of breathing that barely displaces the molecules.

Now, I do indeed love the colors in these pictures but the numbers are regrettably devoid of any significance. For one, math is very hard. It takes me twelve minutes to calculate a proper tip at a restaurant, which is why my wife deals with anything arithmetic-related. But the colors in these pictures are stunning. Truly. You would agree, I'm certain. Blues and greens and reds and yellows that are more vivid and present than you'd believe possible. Humming, like firecrackers captured mid-burst, frozen in paper and ink. To think that those perceived colors are just light with varying wavelengths making all the difference between the sunshine yellows and the icy blues makes me feel small. Who thought of that? It's brilliant—literally. I mean, whoever thought of stars shining is ridiculous. I'm all excited about whoever took these pictures, but whoever blew that thing up to begin with, now Him I've got to meet. If I'm ever in the same room with that Guy, I will not be cool. How could I? And what if our eyes met and I was found out? What if I looked up and saw Him running right at me with His arms spread wide and a torrential smile that would turn dry deserts green? This would be unreasonable. There is no justification for the Dreamer of it all, whom the cosmos and the grass in April and the stream swollen with snowmelt and the baby grabbing your finger and the laugh of kids in kindergarten and the smell of jasmine speak about, to be running toward me. That would be ludicrous. The universe has somewhere around 200,000,000,000 galaxies. In our galaxy alone there are about 100,000,000,000 stars,[17] and there are over 6,000,000,000 people living and breathing right now. Why on earth would He bother coming toward me? I am tiny. I am a dot. Yet here He is with His heart in my chest and we're locked in embrace and I'm not sure exactly when it happened but something fired inside of me, and now my arms are around Him, and people are watching, and I will tell you about it. I don't think I can help it. No more than the stars in a black velvet sky can keep from it.

One attribute of habitual praise is that it is inherent in creation. We tell the glory of God by our very existence. It is unavoidable. We can choose whether to amplify this or not. We can choose to be moved by this or not. Maybe we just need a simple book beside our beds that reminds us of who the household name is. Either way we resound with the heavens, the greatness of the Creator—but when you have met Him, when He has called you His own, then you must open your mouth in response to report this mystery: that the majestic One would come near, would lean in close in all of His glory and embrace us, to mend the division between Him and us. The most famous One of all is concerned with us! Sometimes our awareness of who we are, in light of who He is, is so present and vivid that we become explosions of rescue.

Sometimes praise is impossible to contain. It is a violently full river for which there is no dam high enough or wide enough to contain it. He will be on the tip of our tongue. He will spill out. We will be standing in rooms waiting for others' eyes to meet ours so we can run with a smile that floods and drowns.

# PSALM 19

God's glory is on tour in the skies,
*   God-craft on exhibit across the horizon.*
*   Madame Day holds classes every morning,*
*   Professor Night lectures each evening.*

Their words aren't heard,
*   their voices aren't recorded,*
*   But their silence fills the earth:*
*   unspoken truth is spoken everywhere.*

God makes a huge dome
*   for the sun — a superdome!*
*   The morning sun's a new husband*
*   leaping from his honeymoon bed,*
*   The daybreaking sun an athlete*
*   racing to the tape.*

That's how God's Word vaults across the skies
*   from sunrise to sunset,*
*   Melting ice, scorching deserts,*
*   warming hearts to faith.*

The revelation of GOD is whole
*   and pulls our lives together.*
*   The signposts of GOD are clear*
*   and point out the right road.*
*   The life-maps of GOD are right,*
*   showing the way to joy.*

The directions of GOD are plain
and easy on the eyes.
GOD's reputation is twenty-four-carat gold,
with a lifetime guarantee.
The decisions of GOD are accurate
down to the nth degree.

God's Word is better than a diamond,
    better than a diamond set between emeralds.
    You'll like it better than strawberries in spring,
    better than red, ripe strawberries.

There's more: God's Word warns us of danger
    and directs us to hidden treasure.
    Otherwise how will we find our way?
    Or know when we play the fool?
    Clean the slate, God, so we can start the day fresh!
    Keep me from stupid sins,
    from thinking I can take over your work;
    Then I can start this day sun-washed,
    scrubbed clean of the grime of sin.
    These are the words in my mouth;
    these are what I chew on and pray.
    Accept them when I place them
    on the morning altar,
    O God, my Altar-Rock,
    God, Priest-of-My-Altar.

A-Ha World Tour 86-87 AC/DC For Those About To
Rock We Salute You Tour 1982 AC/DC Fly On The Wall
Tour 1986 AC/DC Blow Up Your Video Tour 1987 AC/
DC Ballbreaker World Tour 1996 AC/DC Stiff Upper
Lip Tour 2001 Aerosmith Nine Lives Tour Aerosmith Get
a Grip Tour 93-94 Aerosmith The Permanent Vacation

Tour Alice Cooper The Nightmare Returns Tour 1986 Alice Cooper Raise Your Fist And Yell Tour 1997 Anthrax Spreading The Disease Tour 1986 Anthrax Among The Living Tour 1987 Backstreet Boys Into The Millennium Tour Balaam And The Angel Live Free Or Die World Tour 1988 Bananarama The 1989 World Tour 1989 Barry Manilow Tour Of The World 1998 Barry White Icon World Tour Beach Boys 15 Big Ones Tour 1976 Beach Boys US Tour 1978 Beach Boys In Concert World Tour 1980 Beautiful South The Beautiful South 1999 Tour Big Country The Seer Tour Billy Joel The Bridge Tour Black Sabbath Heaven And Hell Tour 1980 Black Sabbath Mob Rules Tour 1981 Black Sabbath Seventh Star Tour 1986 Black Sabbath Headless Cross Tour 1989 Blondie Parallel Lines Tour 1979 Blur Seaside Tour '95 Bob Dylan Temples In Flames Tour Bob Dylan True Confessions Tour Bobby Brown Don't Be Cruel Tour Bon Jovi Final Countdown '90 with Cinderella/Skid Row Bon Jovi One Wild Night Tour Boyzone A Different Tour 1996 Boyzone The Boys Are Back In Your Town Tour UK 1996 Brian May Another World — The Tour Brian May Back To The Light Tour '93 Brian Setzer The "Here-I-Go-Again-Draggin-16-Guys-Around-The-World!" Tour Britney Spears Oops! I Did It Again Tour 2000 Bruce Springsteen Born In The USA Tour Bruce Springsteen Tunnel Of Love Express Tour Bryan Adams Waking Up The World Tour '92 Bryan Adams 18 Til I Die Tour '97 Bryan Adams So Far So Good Tour Bryan Adams Best Of Me Tour 1999-2001 Bryan Ferry Mamouna World Tour 1995 Budgie Autumn Tour 1978 Budgie Deliver Us From Evil Tour 1982 Chris De Burgh Tour '99 Chris De Burgh Into The Light Europe '86 Tour Chris Rea Dancing With Strangers World Tour Cinderella Long Cold Winter World Tour 1988-89 Cinderella Heartbreak Station European Tour 1991 Cliff Richard The Silver Tour Cliff Richard 30th

Anniversary World Tour Cliff Richard From A Distance Tour 1990 Cliff Richard The Hit List Tour 1994 Coldplay Coldplay Tour 2003 Crosby, Stills, And Nash Allies Tour 1983 Crosby, Stills And Nash Southern Cross Acoustic Tour 1992 Culture Club Cameras Go Crazy Tour 1981 Culture Club Colour By Numbers Tour 1983 David Lee Roth A Little Ain't Enough Tour 1991 David Bowie The Glass Spider Tour David Bowie A Reality Tour David Bowie Serious Moonlight Tour 1983 David Bowie Sound And Vision Tour 1990 Deep Purple Slaves And Masters Tour 1991 Def Leppard The 7-Day Weekend Tour Dina Carrol UK Tour 1994 Dire Straits Communique European Tour 1979 Dire Straits On Every Street Tour 1991 Duran Duran Seven & The Ragged Tiger World Tour '83 Earth Wind & Fire Tour Of The World 1979 Earth Wind & Fire Heritage Tour '90 Elkie Brooks On Tour 1998 Elton John World Tour '85-86 Elton John Back In The USSA American Tour 1979 Elton John The Big Picture Tour Elvis Costello The Beloved Entertainer Tour 1989 Elvis Costello And The Attractions A Tour To Trust 1981 Elvis Costello Brutal Youth Tour 1994 Elvis Costello Costello Sings Again UK 1996 Elvis Presley The Concert World Tour 1998-2000 Erasure Wild! Tour '89-90 Eric Clapton And His Band North American Tour 1979 Eric Clapton USA Spring Tour 1992 Eric Clapton Money And Cigarettes Tour 1993 Eric Clapton Behind The Sun Tour 1985 Europe The Final Countdown Tour 1987 Eurythmics Touch Tour Eurythmics The Revenge Tour Extreme Stop The World Tour III Fleetwood Mac Behind The Mask Gabrielle Dreams Can Come True Tour 2001 Gary Moore Victims Of The Future World Tour '84 Gary Numan Exhibition Tour 1987 Gary Numan Metal Rhythm Tour 1988 Gary Numan The Fury Tour 1985 Genesis And Then There Were Three Tour 1978 Genesis Abacab Tour 1981 Genesis Invisible Tour

1986 Genesis We Can't Dance Tour 1992 Genesis
Calling All Stations Tour 1998 George Michael The
Faith Tour 1988 Gloria Estefan Into The Light World Tour
1991 Guns And Roses Use Your Illusion Tour 1993 Hall
& Oates H$_2$O Tour 1982 Heart Bad Animals Tour 1988
Heart Brigade World Tour '90 INXS Calling All Nations
Tour 1988 Iron Maiden Fear Of The Dark Tour 1992
Iron Maiden Seventh Tour Of A Seventh Tour 1988
Jamiroquai Synkronized Tour Janet Jackson All For You
World Tour 2002 Janet Jackson World Tour '93-95 Jeff
Beck Rockupation '78 Jethro Tull North American Tour
'78 Johnny Cash The Johnny Cash Show '70 Journey
Frontiers Tour '83 Judas Priest The Painkiller Tour 90-91
K. D. Lang All You Can Eat Tour Kansas Rockupation
Tour '80 King Crimson THRAK '95 Tour Kylie Minogue
Enjoy Yourself UK Tour Laurie Anderson Mister
Heartbreak '84 Lenny Kravitz Circus Tour Lightning
Seeds Dizzy Heights Tour Lisa Loeb Acoustic Solo Tour
Luther Vandross Never Let Me Go On Tour '93-94 Macy
Gray On How Life Is Tour Madonna Blond Ambition
World Tour Marillion Fugazi Tour '84 Metallica Kill 'Em
All For One Tour 1983 Metallica Wherever I May Roam
Tour 91-93 Metallica Nowhere Else To Roam Tour 1993
Metallica Summer Sanitarium Meat Loaf And The
Neverland Express On Tour Meat Loaf Born To Rock
World Tour Michael Bolton The One Thing Tour Michael
Jackson History World Tour Michelle Branch Are You
Happy Now? Tour Mick Taylor Rock Guitar Express '90
Midge Ure The Gift Tour '85 Modern Talking Back For
Good Tour '98 Motley Crue Anywhere USA Tour '81
Motley Crue Cruesing Through Canada Tour 1982
Motley Crue Shout At The Devil Tour '83 Motley Crue
Theater of Pain Tour 1985 Motley Crue Girls, Girls, Girls
World Tour '87-88 Motley Crue Dr Feelgood World
Tour '89 Neil Diamond The Best Years Of Our Lives '97

Neil Diamond World Tour 2001-2002 Neil Young Trans World Tour Ozzy Osbourne Bark At The Moon World Tour '84 Pat Metheny We Live Here World Tour '95 Paul McCartney The Paul McCartney World Tour Paul Young The '9' Go Mad With Davy Crockett World Tour '85 Paul Young '85 Christmas Tour Pink Floyd World Tour 87-88 Pink Floyd Momentary Lapse Of Reason Tour Pink Floyd Animals Tour Poison Flesh and Blood Tour '90 Prince Lovesexy Tour '88 Prince And The N.P.G. World Tour '90 Queensryche The Warning Tour Queensryche Promised Land Tour '95 Radiohead Anyone Can Play Guitar Tour '93 Radiohead Pablo Honey Tour '93 Radiohead Pop Is Dead Tour '93 Radiohead The Bends Tour '95 R.E.O. Speedwagon Good Trouble Tour Reliant K Back To The Few Tour, Reliant K Everybody Wants To Rule The World Tour Ricky Martin Livin' La Vida Loca World Tour Ringo Star Allstar Band Tour '89 Robert Plant The Principal Of Moments Tour '83 Robert Plant Non Stop Go Tour '88 Robert Plant Manic Nirvana Tour '90 Robert Palmer World Tour '92 Rolling Stones Licks World Tour REM Monster Tour '95 Sammy Hagar Live Loud And Clear Tour 1980 Santana Supernatural Tour Saxon Rock The Nations Tour 86-87 Scorpions Savage Amusement Tour '88 Shakira Tour De La Mangosta Shirley Bassey The World's Greatest Female Entertainer UK and Scandanavian Tour '87 Shirley Bassey The Millennium Tour 2000 Simple Minds Good News From The Next World Simply Red The Spirit Of Life Tour Steely Dan Art Crimes '96 Steve Winwood Roll With It Tour '88 Stevie Nicks The Wild Heart Tour Stevie Wonder Hotter Than July Tour '80 Sting Nothing Like The Sun World Tour Sting Mercury Falling Tour Sting The Soul Cages Tour Supertramp It's About Time World Tour '97 Suzanne Vega World Tour '87 Ted Nugent Frenzoid Tour '80 The Cult Ceremonial Stomp World Tour 91-92

The Cure The Prayer Tour The Cure The Dream Tour The
Eagles Tour '76 The Eagles Hell Freezes Over Tour '98
The Police Reggatta De Blanc Tour '79 The Police Ghost
In The Machine Tour 81-82 The Police Rockupation '80
The Police Syncronicity '83 The Shadows Silver
Anniversary World Tour Tina Turner Wildest Dreams
Tour Tom Petty Long After Dark European Tour '82 Tom
Petty Touring The Great Wide Open 91-92 Toto
Rockupation '82 Toto Reunion Concert '99 U2 War Tour
Spring '83 U2 Zooropa Tour U2 Elevation Tour Wham
The Big Tour Whitney Houston I'm Your Baby Tonight
Tour '91 Whitney Houston Moment Of Truth Tour '88
Whitesnake Ready An' Willing Tour '80 Whitesnake
Saints And Sinners Tour 82-83 Whitesnake Return Of
The Snake Tour 1987-88 Whitesnake Greatest Hits Tour
'94 The Who The Witchdoctor Tour 1970s The Who
Faces Dance Tour '81 The Who It's Hard Tour '82
Winger In The Heart Of The Young Tour '91 Yes
Symphonic Tour 2001 Yes The Big Tour '88 (Insert Band
Name) Japan Tour (Insert Year)

Names of tours make me smile. I picture band members sitting around in painfully intense thought. There is silence. There is the tapping of fingers. There are eruptions and lulls. Then the moment of inspiration hits; the air in the room changes. You can just feel it, a detonation of agreement. Idioms of concurrence are roared to convey the same sentiment: "That rocks!" High fives turn into ceremonial pumping handshakes involving both hands and intricate thumb placements and the interlocking of fingers followed by the half hug and back slap.

"Yeah man! ROCKUPATION 1995! That kicks! It's brilliant! Like OCCUPATION but you just change a letter! Freakin' awesome!"

"Actually you change several letters."

"Whatever, man. Don't start with me. Just 'cause it was my idea!"

"Dude, it was so not your idea. I said it right when we sat down, but no one would listen!"

"Whatever, man. You've always got to be the dude. Are you listening to me? Hey, do not turn your back. You know how I get when you turn your back. Are you listening? You hear what I said? 'Cause *I* said it!"

"You don't even know how to spell *occupation*."

"I don't need to man 'cause it's ROCKUPATION! ROCKUPATION, man!"

"No! It's ROCKUPATION 1995!"

"Yeah! Sweet!"

"Hey. Rock and roll!"

More high fives all around and more half hugs that are awkwardly conscious of personal space. Of course *ROCKUPATION 1995* doesn't happen, due to creative differences during rehearsals, so we wait without complaint for THE REUNION TOUR. Oh please, oh please.

But sometimes the magic does happen and a band you're keen on invents a tour name that drips of hip. And can you believe it? They're "coming to a city near you." Tickets are purchased, the wait begins, and anticipation builds. People lose grip on reason over this stuff. They'll drive for days to see the right band in the right room, hoping that a delightful night will unfold, a transcendent experience will transpire. Now and again it actually does.

I love the way the translation of this psalm starts out: "God's glory is on tour in the skies."

How does this sound?

The Glory of God on Tour

Coming to wherever you are. Appearing nightly. Just pay attention. Do you not see the star-shine? Can you see them — glitter flung, humming against the black? Do you not feel the moonlight? Pay attention. How about in the early morning when the breeze is cool and the sun erupts from the horizon, leaking orange and red and yellow everywhere? What about its relentless path scoring the blue-sky air with radiance indefinable? What about the way it gives up, liquid like, melting into evening at the end of every day? You should drive for miles to see this! And the rivers and oceans and the mountains and the trees and the snow and the thunder: all a part of God on Tour. I love that.

Most of us have had the experience of looking at glorious scenery, a beautiful sunset, the pounding of waves, or some similar aspect of nature and of knowing that this could be no accident but must be the work of a Being so awe-inspiring that our only reaction can be, "My God!" At the time this psalm was written, though, it was very common pagan practice to worship nature, to deify the sun and moon and trees and spring and summer and anything else that might wield a decent god name. Unredeemed humanity often has difficulty seeing the Creator in the creation because of its fallen state. So the second half of this passage clearly defines what's on tour here. The flyer tacked to the telephone pole indicating who is headlining the bill says it's the glory of the God of Israel, the Giver of the Law that holds all things together. It is the one true God spoken of in the books of Moses, the Torah, the very *word* of God. It is better than diamonds. The writer of this psalm finds the Maker in the creation and also in the very commands of God, His written Word.

Can we stare into Scripture with as much love? Are we really to find the Law of the Lord as good as sunshine? What would it look like if we finally understood why David couldn't quit talking about the greatness of God's laws? I'm not certain, but if we're having difficulty grasping this, we're not alone. God had to wrap the Law in skin and bones and have it come stare us in the face for us to "get it." He had to give us pictures of the Law redefined—of the Law bringing healing to the afflicted, help to the helpless, and love to the least.

The first half of this psalm finds the Maker mingled in the

created things, and the second portion reveals Him in the Law, in His written Word.

How does this sound as another possible advert?

The Glory of God on Tour

Coming to wherever you are. Appearing in Scripture as His very Word. Read how He takes nothing and makes everything. Let words like "and it was good" devastate you because you know what's coming. Listen as He asks Eve, "What is this that you have done?" and stumble upon yourself. Listen as we try to find our way back and as some get so close to Him that they walk right off the face of this world. Watch as creation strays so far, water covers most of us until we can no longer breathe the air. Then feel delight as light, split into every color, streams from skies warm again with promise. Page after page unfolding the story of rescue and redemption, of reclamation and hope, of the setting right of the world: all a part of God on Tour. I love that.

We are given glimpses of the Creator in starlight and Scripture.

I understand what it is to look at nature, and I say, "My God!" because I've seen the Creator. I look into black skies strewn with shimmering dots of light—nights that buzz with word of their Maker. Moonlight you can feel on your skin if you pay really close attention some October evening, a touch of remembrance that the sun is shining just as bright as ever and dawn is coming. Brilliant drops of rain that sing His name all the way down their journey from cloud to dirt. Grass you can feel growing underfoot if you're really still.

And what of this paper and ink, these pages of divine breath? These words are like treasure. They hold the Christ I know. They are the pulse of the God who created, the One who came and the One I call friend, the One whose presence is here and accessible, the One who rescues me and keeps rescuing me. It holds the jewels of our plight. Here are the stories of our running and His running after.

What we praise signifies our treasure. Let love for God's Word fall from our mouths and drip from our lives.

# PSALM 29

Bravo, G<small>OD</small>, bravo!
  Gods and all angels shout, "Encore!"
  In awe before the glory,
  in awe before God's visible power.
  Stand at attention!
  Dress your best to honor him!

G<small>OD</small> thunders across the waters,
  Brilliant, his voice and his face, streaming brightness —
  G<small>OD</small>, across the flood waters.

G<small>OD</small>'s thunder tympanic,
  G<small>OD</small>'s thunder symphonic.

G<small>OD</small>'s thunder smashes cedars,
  G<small>OD</small> topples the northern cedars.

The mountain ranges skip like spring colts,
  The high ridges jump like wild kid goats.

G<small>OD</small>'s thunder spits fire.
  G<small>OD</small> thunders, the wilderness quakes;
  He makes the desert of Kadesh shake.

G<small>OD</small>'s thunder sets the oak trees dancing
  A wild dance, whirling; the pelting rain strips their
    branches.
  We fall to our knees — we call out, "Glory!"

Above the floodwaters is GOD's throne
from which his power flows,
from which he rules the world.

GOD makes his people strong.
GOD gives his people peace.

This is a song of thunder. This is a song of transcendent holiness. This is a song of dancing trees and running mountains.

Short-term memory is mystifying. I don't want to take up too much of our time together with a lengthy critique of our educational system but I do need to state that it has done a fair job of helping me develop my short-term memory into an incredibly efficient machine. Things come and go like lightning. My wife told me to do something this morning. I heard her. She said, "David, I really need you to . . . ," and then there is blackness. Nothing. I have no idea what it could have possibly been. I responded, "No problem. Done." But here I am and there is nothingness. This happens every day.

There are times I am driving my car and things seem to start out okay but then five or ten minutes across town I can't recall where I was heading, so I wander the city aimlessly until the original destination floats back into my head or I find someplace else I'm convinced is equally intriguing. It sounds a small bit crazy to say out loud, and I would feel a little vulnerable in the sharing of this were it not for friends who have similar experiences. So, on their and my behalf, there must be blame displacement. It is required. *It must be the educational system.* This institution has trained my brain to store and retrieve information in such a way as to waste my gasoline and bring the fury of my wife upon me. It is their fault, I am certain, this mind that is coated with some sort of slick repellent. If I could just get things to stick. It's like shooting those red suction darts against a window. You shoot, it sticks, and then you watch and you know it's going to loosen its grip and drop to the floor at any second . . . you wait . . . watching as the air acts upon the seal with persistence, coercing space between glass and rubber . . . and there it goes, plunging lifelessly to the floor. No matter how much you lick it or clean the window or increase your proximity to the target before pulling the trigger, it falls away. Things just don't stick.

One of my more frustrating experiences with this was in my study of trees. For two years I considered myself an arborist. It began while I was watching a John Wayne movie. One of the characters said resolutely with a pound of his fist to the table where he was seated, "I'm gonna move there and sink me in some roots." It is extraordinary where threads of thought can lead you. In that small moment I became fixated on the word *roots* for some reason. I scanned my brain to see if there was any information regarding roots. For a while there wasn't much other than a movie of that title that was on TV back in the '80s. I watched all of it. It was really long. Then I tried to recall other mini-series of equal length. There was *The Thorn Birds,* there was a sci-fi series where aliens came to earth asking for help and a few suspicious humans discovered their horrific true intentions and prepared to resist. *V The Final Chapter,* I believe it was called, and then all of a sudden this picture flashed inside my head:

What? Roots as deep and as wide as the winter branches above the ground? This couldn't be possible! How? I had to know more. Where was the rest of the information that should have come with this picture? If the *picture* had been buried in my head, then the other stuff had to be in there as well. But where? Much more blame displacement was needed to explain the absence of this data.

So I went and bought some books. I bought stacks of books. Books about trees. For two years, I thought about trees. For two years I talked about trees. I fell in love with trees. Trees with branches stretching out in tangled webs covered in Spanish moss. Green Firs stretching straight up mountainsides investigating limits in elevation. Pine trees, Spruce trees, Cedars, Ashes, Maples, Catalpas, Walnuts, Pecans, Hickories, Sumacs, Sycamores, Sweetgums, Redbuds, Poplars, Aspens, Cottonwoods, Oaks, Beeches, Birches, Elms, Alders, Palms—all of them I loved. I carried a tree book in my back pocket. It soon wore out, and I bought another one. Friends sometimes found my study an inconvenience, like when I would wander off mid-conversation into suburban forests, eyes trained on something demanding attention, with tree book in hand. Driving became hazardous, too, as I would pull the book out in search of something I had just passed. It took forever to get anywhere. There were so many trees and so many pages to match them with. For two years my peers put up with my monologues about simple, compound, feather compound, fan compound, twice compound leaves alternate or opposite, lobed or toothed, broad or needle-like.

And now there is nothing. I can't remember a thing about trees. The book is no longer in my pocket, and the details are no longer consciously retrievable. It's there, I know it, but I just can't find it. One thing I do know, and can speak certain of, is there was never anything about trees dancing. There was nothing about dancing in the little pocket book I carried. There was nothing about dancing in the thick books on my shelf. There were no pictures of "dancing trees" in the book on my coffee table. No. There was no dancing. None.

In Psalm 29, though, there *are* trees that dance. What in the world? Are these the spooky trees with the long-fingered, gnarly branch hands that grow in the dark, spooky forest and grab up little children unfortunate enough to wander by? No. These tree dancers are more likely to be cast in that John Wayne movie. They're more akin to the poor dude forced into his little jig by bullets flying underfoot not far from a guy in a black hat, laughing maniacally, pistol in hand. It seems these trees don't have a choice. Their Maker has spoken with thunder and wind and electricity. The glory of God is on display, and animation is the result.

In Texas, we sit on porches and watch thunderstorms roll in. You see them coming from a long way off, black and menacing with bursts of light inside the clouds. You count the seconds between the flash and the sound of air splitting in two to tell how far away the storm is.

FLASH!

"One, two, three, four, five . . . "

BANG!

"One mile."

Then the storm would suddenly be on you with strength to rip trees from the ground. To pull them up. To bend them over. Roots as vast as branches in winter that sway and twist, and they still don't have a chance. This is the dancing we're talking about. This is no waltz. It is frenzy and fire. It is *breaking* set to the furious music of wind and rain.

"In awe before the glory, in awe before God's visible power."

I think we might have stored the holiness of God in short-term memory. We shoot the dart against the wall every once in a while, but it always just falls away. We have such lovely intentions at times and turn the vehicle down that road, and then we forget we were heading to the feet of a king. We've become uncomfortably numb to the truth that our destination is the feet of the Holy *Other-Than* Transcendent Creator King of All Heaven and Earth. We are numb and uncomfortably content. We've built churches and sermons to make Him tame and accessible, to make Him seem approachable as one who fits neatly into our lives, and we forget that His is the voice of thunder and lightning. Our comfort is unsettling. It is an uncomfortable comfort. We have bedsores. Our skin itches. From the inside. We know there is more to the story than just Christ, who is this God with this skin that we have gotten so chummy with. We speak easily of Jesus as our pal—our friend who comes to us on bended knee to wash feet and bring hugs—but we forget, with little difficulty, that it was God's justice, the necessity of His holiness, that brought death to give life. It is His holiness that required the shedding of blood, the losing of life, to be the only way to make things right. It was the turning of His back that darkened the sky as our Christ breathed finality.

Maybe we need to bury ourselves in His transcendence to realize there's as much of His just vengeance buried under the ground as this love we so effortlessly talk about. He sets trees dancing. He sends mountains running. This psalm is a hymn of His thunder.

This is a hymn of holiness.

And where is this holy God throughout the storm? In this psalm we see the created things quake while He sits above it all. He is where things are right, where things are as they should be. It is His holiness that is bringing us there. His justice that is making the way. "We fall to our knees—we call out, 'Glory!'" Sometimes praise comes face to the ground, unable to move because we are so aware that this holy, terrifying God has busied Himself bringing us back to Him.

Let the knowledge of His transcendence bring us back to life. Let it flow like blood to sleeping limbs, and feel them tingle as they awake in awe. Shake life back into your hands and let them clap of His goodness. Shake life back into your legs and let them carry you running with wind and thunder. Shake life back into your chest and let your heart beat in pounding reverence. Let praise come face to the ground, trembling with life and awareness that we are found by a holy God.

 # PSALM 40

I waited and waited and waited for GOD.
At last he looked; finally he listened.
He lifted me out of the ditch,
pulled me from deep mud.
He stood me up on a solid rock
to make sure I wouldn't slip.
He taught me how to sing the latest God-song,
a praise-song to our God.
More and more people are seeing this:
they enter the mystery,
abandoning themselves to GOD.

Blessed are you who give yourselves over to GOD,
turn your backs on the world's "sure thing,"
ignore what the world worships;
The world's a huge stockpile
of GOD-wonders and God-thoughts.
Nothing and no one
comes close to you!
I start talking about you, telling what I know,
and quickly run out of words.
Neither numbers nor words
account for you.

Doing something for you, bringing something to you —
that's not what you're after.
Being religious, acting pious —
that's not what you're asking for.

You've opened my ears
so I can listen.

So I answered, "I'm coming.
    I read in your letter what you wrote about me,
    And I'm coming to the party
    you're throwing for me."
    That's when God's Word entered my life,
    became part of my very being.

I've preached you to the whole congregation,
    I've kept back nothing, GOD — you know that.
    I didn't keep the news of your ways
    a secret, didn't keep it to myself.
    I told it all, how dependable you are, how thorough.
    I didn't hold back pieces of love and truth
    For myself alone. I told it all,
    let the congregation know the whole story.

Now GOD, don't hold out on me,
    don't hold back your passion.
    Your love and truth
    are all that keeps me together.
    When troubles ganged up on me,
    a mob of sins past counting,
    I was so swamped by guilt
    I couldn't see my way clear.
    More guilt in my heart than hair on my head,
    so heavy the guilt that my heart gave out.

Soften up, GOD, and intervene;
    hurry and get me some help,
    So those who are trying to kidnap my soul
    will be embarrassed and lose face,
    So anyone who gets a kick out of making me miserable

will be heckled and disgraced,
So those who pray for my ruin
will be booed and jeered without mercy.

But all who are hunting for you —
oh, let them sing and be happy.
Let those who know what you're all about
tell the world you're great and not quitting.
And me? I'm a mess. I'm nothing and have nothing:
make something of me.
You can do it; you've got what it takes —
but God, don't put it off.

This psalm is like an episode of *Gilligan's Island*. Seriously. I think I need you to sing along. Like you mean it. Yes, for real. I know you're there on your plane heading back to Georgia, sitting next to the guy you just met who sells medical equipment, or there in your kitchen sipping coffee on a Monday morning while the rest of the world sleeps, or perhaps just thumbing through this thing in the bookstore, but I think you're going to feel better if you sing. Yes, about everything. Okay, so on three. One. Two. Come on, nice and loud! THREE.

Just sit right back and you'll hear a tale, a tale of a fateful trip, that started from this tropic port, aboard this tiny ship.

The mate was a mighty sailin' man, the Skipper brave and sure. Five passengers set sail that day for a three hour tour. A three hour tour.

The weather started getting rough, the tiny ship was tossed. If not for the courage of the fearless crew, the Minnow would be lost. The Minnow would be lost.

The ship set ground on the shore of this uncharted desert isle,

with Gilligan, the Skipper too,
the Millionaire and his wife,
the *movie* star, the Professor and
Mary Ann, here on Gilligan's Isle![18]

You did not sing. In your head does not count. When you were ten, you would have done it. You left me alone and there were a lot more syllables to fit in than I remember. Again with the pesky short-term memory. I, however, do still recall the *Gilligan's Island* formula for such a successful and truly insightful commentary on the human condition. It goes like this: A problem arises. A headhunter, a gorilla, or something equally as terrifying, such as quicksand, comes along and intrudes into the lives of our deserted-isle protagonists, but within the thirty allotted minutes things are back in order. The episodes with the quicksand would keep me from sleep when I was a child. They would play in my young mind while I stared into dark and weighed the consequences of a trip to my parent's room to ask questions. I was constantly poking mud, convinced it could be of the same constitution as that part of the island holding this bit of earth that is dirt and water mixed in deadly proportion. To wander into it brings the surety of sinking. To fight the sinking simply causes the horrific predicament to be exacerbated. Here, I drew you a map so you can see where the quicksand is.

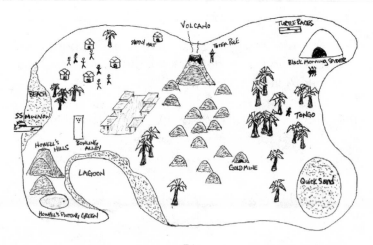

This was terrifying to me. In one episode the quicksand almost snared Lord Beasley as he chased after a Pussycat Swallowtail—the rarest butterfly in the world. This deepest-mass-of-loose-wet-sand was wholly impartial in its swallowing. It sucked down everything, from wildlife to Mr. Howell's suitcase. The quicksand was to be feared. Once, the castaways went in search of the millionaire. He had disappeared. They tracked pieces of his apparel strewn about the island and were shocked to discover his hat floating on a quick-sand pit. A traumatic moment to say the least. Filled with sorrow, the castaways held an impressive funeral service, eulogizing their lost friend. Meanwhile, Mr. Howell watched in bewilderment from atop a nearby tree.

Thankfully, as always, things were resolved by half-hour's end. But the islanders were still stuck. They were still imprisoned on that island. There were always two rescues we were hoping for. One was from the gorilla or big-game hunter or savage visitors from other islands or the allergies plaguing the Skipper or the horrific decision of deputizing Gilligan or the compulsive kidnapper Don Rickles . . . or the quicksand. But the other rescue for which we were rooting was the bigger tale. It was the one that kept us coming back to join the castaways week after week. We begged for them to get a glimpse of something on the horizon so we could watch them start a fire or spell something in rocks on the beach. They didn't belong on the island, and we wanted things to be put right.

I love the Psalms because they are prayers of real people. We find ourselves in them. The stuff of life happens and this is how they (and we) respond. The stuff of God happens and this is how they (and we) respond. These collected words give examples of how the two fit together. How life unfolds and you find God in the middle of it all. I am confident that Psalm 40 is as universal a prayer as ever there was. The passage begins with "God help me!" Then we read of rescue and thanksgiving directed to a listening Savior. But by the end of this psalm we're back to "God help me!" The cyclical repetition of storm and release, tempest and calm. Things are fine, then one foot loses hold and you feel it slide and you dig harder but it's no use—there's just no traction. Then both feet are churning and you're flinging your arms for balance but your wild movements have only caused you to sink more and now every step is deeper and more foul and the mud's grip grows more sure. You've lost your shoes. You're not even sure when they were torn from you, and the mud is cold and full of sharpness. Now you've got it all over your hands and arms and the more you strive to claw your way out the more stuck you become. But just as hope sinks, you are plucked from it all. You feel firm earth beneath your feet. You feel the mud start to dry and fall away. "Thank you" pours from every pore. Clarity is present in that moment. There is but one place to lay exaltation. You see the whole world as "a huge stockpile of GOD-wonders and God-thoughts." Then just as soon as it seems you have run out of words to express this gratitude you feel your foot begin to slide.

Psalm 40 offers two rescues. The obvious one is found in the plight of its writer and the coming of relief. It is the straightforward assurance that there are many pits and recurring liberations. But then there is the greater story. It might not be glaringly apparent on a first read. (At times the sunshine hides the stars but they are no less there.) You see, this psalm is prophetic. David is permitted a peek at what's coming. Christ is found in these verses. If we haven't already spotted the suffering of Christ in this psalm, then the author of Hebrews 10:5-9 makes it certain. This psalm holds our Jesus. Read as He waits patiently. Patience perfected in a garden. Patience on brutal trial before Herod and Pilate. Is there mire thicker than the beams of a wooden cross and a darkened silent sky? The hidden treasure of Psalm 40 is the beauty of a Savior who has cried our same cry. It holds a Savior who has waited and waited and waited on with faith that the promises of God are sure. Faith that none of God's children wait in vain.

In this, there is comfort. Comfort in the words of the psalmist that say, "I know, I've been there. And listen, our God is faithful. You will not go under. Wait! Just wait. Hold on because He will not forsake you. See, He was faithful and found me. He will find me again. He is coming." *There* is the bigger tale. The ship on the horizon. It is the comfort of Christ. It is the assurance of Jesus and the work He has done. It is the promise that we would not be left alone, that a liberator was coming—has come. It is the promise of rescue. It is transcendent God descending to surely pluck us from the mud but also to share our toil, and in our suffering we share in His. We are reminded that He was once where we are, and He is praised in our awareness. Sometimes praise is repetitively desperate, but it is often in these repetitious cries that purer praise is found. Thanksgiving is inherent in our persistently patient faith.

Consider it a sheer gift, friends, when tests and challenges come at you from all sides. You know that under pressure, your faith-life is forced into the open and shows its true colors. So don't try to get out of anything prematurely. Let it do its work so you become mature and well-developed, not deficient in any way.

— JAMES 1:2-4

 # PSALM 50

The God of gods — it's GOD! — speaks out, shouts,
"Earth!" welcomes the sun in the east,
    farewells the disappearing sun in the west.
    From the dazzle of Zion,
    God blazes into view.
    Our God makes his entrance,
    he's not shy in his coming.
    Starbursts of fireworks precede him.

He summons heaven and earth as a jury,
    he's taking his people to court:
    "Round up my saints who swore
    on the Bible their loyalty to me."

The whole cosmos attests to the fairness of this court,
    that here God is judge.

"Are you listening, dear people? I'm getting ready to
speak;
    Israel, I'm about ready to bring you to trial.
    This is God, your God,
    speaking to you.
    I don't find fault with your acts of worship,
    the frequent burnt sacrifices you offer.
    But why should I want your blue-ribbon bull,
    or more and more goats from your herds?
    Every creature in the forest is mine,
    the wild animals on all the mountains.

I know every mountain bird by name;
the scampering field mice are my friends.
If I get hungry, do you think I'd tell you?
All creation and its bounty are mine.
Do you think I feast on venison?
or drink draughts of goats' blood?
Spread for me a banquet of praise,
serve High God a feast of kept promises,
And call for help when you're in trouble —
I'll help you, and you'll honor me."

Next, God calls up the wicked:
"What are you up to, quoting my laws,
talking like we are good friends?
You never answer the door when I call;
you treat my words like garbage.
If you find a thief, you make him your buddy;
adulterers are your friends of choice.
Your mouth drools filth;
lying is a serious art form with you.
You stab your own brother in the back,
rip off your little sister.
I kept a quiet patience while you did these things;
you thought I went along with your game.
I'm calling you on the carpet, now,
laying your wickedness out in plain sight.

"Time's up for playing fast and
loose with me.
I'm ready to pass sentence,
and there's no help in sight!
It's the praising life that honors me.
As soon as you set your foot on the Way,
I'll show you my salvation."

In junior high, I was quite the jokester. Now I am quite dull, but back then I had routines. Well-rehearsed lines that were sure to retrieve a few chuckles from my classmates. One of my favorite bits was as follows:

First I would spot a group of peers. The larger the better. No less than seven. They were required to be in a disorganized clump but close enough in proximity to one another for the unaided human voice to reach each individual.

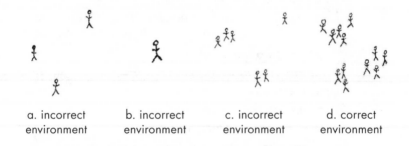

| a. incorrect environment | b. incorrect environment | c. incorrect environment | d. correct environment |

Once I spotted the proper environment I would then project my voice with a weight of importance, indicating the necessity of promptness in response. Some phrases that might be used were *"Hey, come here." "Everyone. Pay attention. Over here." "Come close!" "Closer." "Really, everyone lean in." "Quietly now. Listen." "I have something to say."* After I had ensured complete silence and every eye was locked to mine, I would wait. I would silently look from person to person to person with a slightly approving grin. Inevitably, someone's patience would cease and he or she would say, "What?!" in a raised, aggravated tone. In response, I would allow the grin to grow, to creep over my face, blooming into full smile. Then I, with utmost timing, would unleash the punch line: "I just wanted to be the center of attention."

Of course, then I would receive punches and some small amount of verbal abuse, but it was so worth it. It was always worth it. It never got old. Every time I executed it with passion, and every time they fell for it. The story of some boy crying wolf was lost on me. The moral never hit home. I was sure that this boy doing the crying wasn't passionate enough. He never sold it. I, on the other hand, could sell it every time.

Psalm 50 starts with what must be one of the grandest statements of history. GOD informs us that He is about to speak. And if there is confusion about which god, well it's God the God of gods—GOD. You know, Caps Lock GOD. I'm pretty sure no other gods get the Caps Lock key. When Caps Lock happens it indicates a translating of the personal name of God. The one revealed to Moses at the burning bush. You will see it in some translations as LORD. Caps Lock. Caps Lock GOD doesn't show up to make a meek request, "Um. Excuse me. Uh, okay, I'm about to say a few things, if I could have your attention please." No, this is not what happens. His entrance is huge! He speaks—no, shouts—"Earth!" Whoa. The hair on the back of my neck just stood up. This voice could split you apart. GOD shows up shining, scattering glittered beams everywhere, His magnificent splendor on display. The whole of the heavens are summoned. All of the cosmos is at attention. This is huge! It is our Creator who is about to speak. The One who started this all is about to open His mouth as judge.

He starts the proceedings with good news. He states that He doesn't find fault with Israel's blood sacrifices. But then He begins to question. He asks why He should want them? Did He not create the bull and the goat? Do we think He is hungry and in need of them to feast on? Is He thirsty and the only thing fit to quench such thirst is the blood of a freshly slain lamb? Then after this rhetorical line of questioning, He makes what I think could be a defining statement for our understanding of praise. The sacrifice Caps Lock GOD is looking for . . . praise.

What? Isn't that like calling us all together to say, "Hey, I just wanted to be the center of attention"? Let me try to reframe GOD's address and perhaps make it cut a little more for our moment.

"I don't find fault with your singing of songs. But do you think I'm in great need of music? Do you think it is too quiet where I am? Did I not make the air molecules to vibrate and dance in such a way to let melody float from here to there? Do you think I am in great need of hearing these songs that were my breathings in the first place?"

We may argue, "Isn't that praise? Songs = Praise, right?" I think they're more like burnt offerings. The good news is that GOD doesn't find fault with our song offerings. There's nothing wrong with them. In fact, they can be beautiful expressions. But often they're nothing more than ritual, and at their worst they can even be provoking to GOD. Well then, what is He looking for? What is this praise He's after? It is Praise Living. It is GOD leaning in and shouting, "I am the center!" and the sum of our lives nodding back in agreement. It is the core of our hearts echoing this statement. The difference between my juvenile prank and the statement GOD makes is that He speaks the facts. He is not begging to be the center—He *is* the center. He *is* the source. Our songs might verbalize and echo that at times, but so what? It is the nuts and bolts of our living that indicate if we really think this is truth. I would be so bold as to say eating barbecue and wearing the sauce on your fingers and face and a grin as big as Texas with the knowledge that Caps Lock GOD is at the center of this can be truer praise than belting this "song ritual" that we have elevated to dangerous heights.

According to this psalm, even the simplicity of calling out to Him in times of trouble is considered the truer sacrifice. How surprising is that? And how easy? Higher than our ritual is the simple acknowledgment that, in truth, *He* is what we need. We, like the Israelites, often find rescue in the burnt offering and not in the GOD who is the source of all. We find comfort in the song and not in the Comforter. It is a subtle but necessary shift. It is more difficult to find the Creator in a barbecue sandwich than in your favorite Sunday-morning song, but when you do, when you begin to find Him in all the stuff of life, everything starts singing. Every moment breaks into song. Every breath becomes sacrifice, and the songs become sweetness. This is living praise.

PSALM 63

God — you're my God!
    I can't get enough of you!
    I've worked up such hunger and thirst for God,
    traveling across dry and weary deserts.

So here I am in the place of worship, eyes open,
    drinking in your strength and glory.
    In your generous love I am really living at last!
    My lips brim praises like fountains.
    I bless you every time I take a breath;
    My arms wave like banners of praise to you.

I eat my fill of prime rib and gravy;
    I smack my lips. It's time to shout praises!
    If I'm sleepless at midnight,
    I spend the hours in grateful reflection.
    Because you've always stood up for me,
    I'm free to run and play.
    I hold on to you for dear life,
    and you hold me steady as a post.

Those who are out to get me are marked for doom,
    marked for death, bound for hell.
    They'll die violent deaths;
    jackals will tear them limb from limb.
    But the king is glad in God;
    his true friends spread the joy,
    While small-minded gossips
    are gagged for good.

Now, of all the barbecue I've eaten in my lifetime, Texas has the best. Of course, I live in Texas—Waco, Texas, to be exact—but I've truly tried to be objective. Waco is just about as Texas as it comes. It's located an hour and a half south of Dallas and an hour and a half north of Austin. It's smack in the middle of the state. So much so that our city asserts the slogan "The Heart of Texas." I don't know who is responsible for the calculations or how we're able to make such a claim, but we have. It is written on our billboards and our water towers. It is printed on the brochures at rest stops. It must be truth because the coliseum that houses the rodeo during our October county fair is named "The Heart of Texas Coliseum." So in all biasness I'm here to assert that we have the best barbecue on the planet. Not that Memphis or Kansas City pork nonsense. This is Texan cattle smoked over Texan lumber. On Franklin Avenue very near to my house there is a barbecue joint that has a smoker in the shape of a pistol. For real. A giant pistol. It is huge. You could put a whole cow in the chamber, which is indeed where the meat goes. The smoke exits the gun from the barrel end. It is complete optical and olfactory stimulation to be near when it is fired. And they cater. The pistol has a hitch. They haul the pistol smoker wherever there is the need for smoking cattle. I've eaten barbecue from all over and nothing beats the pistol. You doubt me? Behold the pistol:

The pistol is beauty. You must taste meat from the pistol. You will hug me and tell me how your life has been changed for the better.[19]

I love Psalm 63. It is one of the most beautifully inspiring passages in the entire Psalter. And I really love Eugene Peterson's translation of it. Other translations have a dark, forbidding, weightiness to them. In *The Message* we eavesdrop on David's desert lament and almost forget that he is without his usual creature comforts. His mystical satisfaction in the things of God virtually leads us to believe he is in want of nothing. I remember reading it for the first time and the thought passed through my head, *I bet David would have loved Texas slow-smoked brisket.* Anyone who is in a desert and starts going on about prime rib and comparing it to feasting on God would love Texas barbecue.

This psalm is supposed to be a lament, but you can feel joy buried here. Most likely this was written while David was on the run from his son Absalom.[20] He has forfeited his crown, his palace, his honors, the hearts of his people, and the love of his child, whom he cared for completely. The psalmist is alone with God. In his hour of desolation he looks up to heaven. And even here in the desert, song erupts from him. Song of hungry, thirsty, violent, sleepless praise. With God as audience it seems nothing is out of bounds. Here there is room for it all. The astounding thing is that David almost makes Job look like a whiner. Credit must be placed where credit is due, and certainly credit is due here. Here is example made. Here is inspiration. And here, too, is evaluation, for us. In the desert, what is it we beg for? It seems a vicious and familiar trend of God to lead His own into wildernesses. Usually, we look around and see nothing but sand while anger rises inside. We think we should be anywhere but the middle of heat and dust. The wind is harsh and stings with silt. Sand is getting in our socks and dirtying our ankles as it mixes with our sweat.

We always assume that the desert is not where we belong. Perhaps it was too subtle, but if we would have paid attention we might have felt His hand with delicate softness take ours, and our fingers slowly interlock, and then the gentle pull away from the green grass and the mountain springs. We might have seen that we did not wander here alone. Instead we fling ourselves about as if no one were aware of our desperate location. Look at David. He does not cry, "I thirst for water," but "I thirst for You." He does not cry, "I thirst for the blood of my enemies" or "I thirst for deliverance from this desert land where there's no water" or "I thirst for my crown, my kingdom, my son, my due," but "I thirst and hunger for You." The only thing suitably quenching is the nearness of God.

What would it be like if joy in the desert were as natural as our love for barbecue on a Texas Sunday afternoon in the middle of August? What would it be like to know without question that God is as present on the floor of the canyon as He is on the crest of the hill? To have this confident hope buried deep in our bones. To know no other than our Savior and feel the soul scream, "This is enough! I need no more than You! You are a feast! You are a cool spring! You are deliverance! You are a balm for all wounds! Your near presence is everything! It is breath! It is Life!"

 PSALM 66

All together now — applause for God!
    Sing songs to the tune of his glory,
    set glory to the rhythms of his praise.
    Say of God, "We've never seen anything like him!"
    When your enemies see you in action,
    they slink off like scolded dogs.
    The whole earth falls to its knees —
    it worships you, sings to you,
    can't stop enjoying your name and fame.

Take a good look at God's wonders —
    they'll take your breath away.
    He converted sea to dry land;
    travelers crossed the river on foot.
    Now isn't that cause for a song?

Ever sovereign in his high tower, he keeps
    his eye on the godless nations.
    Rebels don't dare
    raise a finger against him.

Bless our God, O peoples!
    Give him a thunderous welcome!
    Didn't he set us on the road to life?
    Didn't he keep us out of the ditch?
    He trained us first,
    passed us like silver through refining fires,
    Brought us into hardscrabble country,

pushed us to our very limit,
Road-tested us inside and out,
took us to hell and back;
Finally he brought us
to this well-watered place.

I'm bringing my prizes and presents to your house.
I'm doing what I said I'd do,
What I solemnly swore I'd do
that day when I was in so much trouble:
The choicest cuts of meat
for the sacrificial meal;
Even the fragrance
of roasted lamb is like a meal!
Or make it an ox
garnished with goat meat!

All believers, come here and listen,
let me tell you what God did for me.
I called out to him with my mouth,
my tongue shaped the sounds of music.
If I had been cozy with evil,
the Lord would never have listened.
But he most surely did listen,
he came on the double when he heard my prayer.
Blessed be God: he didn't turn a deaf ear,
he stayed with me, loyal in his love.

This Psalm is said to be recited on Easter day, by the Greek church: it is described in the Greek Bible as A Psalm of the Resurrection.

— DANIEL CRESSWELL[21]

Easter has to be one of the more meaningful days of the year for those of the Christian faith. It is the celebration of Life's triumph, the accomplishment of reparation and release. I remember as a child asking my parents why there were so many more people at church.

I remember new Sunday clothes. I remember discovering that white shoes were somehow appropriate on this day but an embarrassment before it. I would ask for this information to be repeated every year as I was truly intrigued by it.

"So now everyone can wear white shoes, huh, Mom?"

"Yes. You are right. Everyone can now wear their white shoes and white hose."

I never could remember when white shoes became embarrassing again, but every Easter I knew that there would be full pews and folks wearing hats who usually didn't wear hats and lots of white shoes—oh, and that my mom tended to cry more easily on that morning than other Sundays.

At an early age I began to make some sense out of the story line of my faith that was emerging as we fixedly recalled and reenacted portions of it surrounding this particular Sunday of the year. But I've yet to get my head about the rest of the Easter hoopla. For one, the colors are horrible. Pastels never work. Well, they seldom work. They do come together quite brilliantly in certain beach towns frozen in the tackier colors of 1981, but for the most part they should really be left alone. It is an unfortunate palette merger to say the least, and for some horrible reason this holiday is stuck with it. Have you seen those "Easter Trees"? I find it impossible to remain in a room with one. I have tried, really I have, but it is just too painful to watch.

For me, the real fear surrounding this day was the bunny. I couldn't work out what the eggs had to do with the bunny. Why would a bunny leave eggs? And then I couldn't figure out the principle of the bunny's powers. Santa I understood because he was like me. Well, larger and older with a certain smell of peppermint that I did not have, but human nonetheless. A human with flying deer and elves. I could cope with this. I understood how he could disseminate all of the gifts in one night because he had such fabulous help and of course flew in the opposite direction of the earth's rotation. But the bunny? This was ridiculous. Early on, I concluded that the eggs were not actually *his* and that there must be more than one of him. But on a fundamental level, I was just frightened by the role of bunnies at Easter. Especially as I watched my friends get an Easter bunny on this day—a real one—as a pet. This made no sense. You didn't get a Santa for Christmas. I would watch carefully as my friends' new bunnies hopped about the very yard we were supposed to be running around in and finding the eggs that one of these evil bunnies had supposedly hidden. I would stand silently with my basket hanging at my side, full of eggs I had already spied and retrieved or stealthily stolen from the other kids' baskets when they weren't looking, all the while staring intently into the eyes of each bunny, wondering which one was the culprit. Whose eggs were these, and which bunny was dumb enough to think a pink egg lying in the fat middle of a green lawn qualifies as "hidden"? They were *all* suspect. None of them would look me in the eye for very long, and they all looked the same. See, look. Here are four bunnies. You tell me which one is "the" Easter bunny.

a.   b.   c.   d.

It's just impossible. Santa is not this sneaky or ambiguous.

And what was with the giving of little baby chicks? The thought would come to me while lying in bed in the dark that my friend who received a little blue baby chick on Easter two years ago did not now own a full-grown blue chicken. In fact, I hadn't seen any type of chicken running around his house. I usually made plans to investigate this further but the thought was gone by morning and thus it remains just one more bit of evidence that folks were simply out of good colors and good ideas when they decided what to do with the marketing of Easter for commercial purposes. Peeps are another example of this holiday's misfortune. "Hey, let's take a marshmallow and cover it in granulated sugar and give it to people to eat" (see appendix D).

The beauty of holidays has a lot to do with communal nostalgia. There is often a gathering of family and friends and amid that, a communal remembering. A retelling of "the last time we were together" or a remembering and telling of what has transpired in our lives since we last sat in the same room. Around Christmas and Easter there is also much communal remembering about our faith. This is a good and necessary thing. We need more moments like this, where we gather and retell our story of rescue. Where we, with intentionality like the psalmist's, call all to "take a good look at God's wonders."

In remembering our rescue, we remember life. This psalm celebrates that. It celebrates the wonder of what God has done and recalls our faithfulness to Him. It articulates God's actions and our sacrificial response. It articulates our movement from bondage and exile to the promised place of freedom. After the pleading, after passing through fire, after the desert, there is the well-watered place. And it is, for us, a lesson in how to respond appropriately to life, to this light that has broken in, to this marvelous rescue. This song teaches us to remember, to recall and retell our liberation. In our remembering, there is revealing, and where there is revealing, there is opportunity for reveling response. And when our rescue is deep, when it is from a place that seemed unreachable, from a place where no light was visible, there is room for much joy, a celebration of movement from death to life.

So how do we respond as community? What is appropriate? How could anything be appropriate? What could we bring that would be sufficient?

We can bring song; we can bring music. This psalm is a song about songs. It revels in the expressive dramatic power of melody and the beauty of our voices mingling in thankfulness. Where rescue is found, so will be found the best "expressers and communicators" we humans have. Art seems to be one of those things. We were created in such a way that music erupts from us when we are squeezed. Whether it is a violent wringing or love's embrace, song drips out. So sing with all your might. Paint with fury. Write words noisy with color. Dance. Dance until we can see your soul. Let remembering squeeze you, then go get a bucket to catch the drippings.

When we are fully aware of rescue, it should also cause us to bring an offering of our best, with the knowledge that we can not respond in equal portion to God's actions but with all that we have available to express our gratefulness for such deliverance. This is a humbling knowing to carry, and we see in this psalm that this humility is an especially appropriate response. We come in breathless wonderment on our knees, and we call the whole of creation to hear and understand what this God of gods has done for us. Sometimes remembering comes in small unexpected and surprising moments, but it is also a vital thing to have these larger moments written in red on the community calendar, to give ourselves fully to that communal remembering, despite the baggage that may come with it, or perhaps, precisely *because* of it.

 # PSALM 74

You walked off and left us, and never looked back.
    God, how could you do that?
    We're your very own sheep;
    how can you stomp off in anger?

Refresh your memory of us — you bought us a long time ago.
    Your most precious tribe — you paid a good price for us!
    Your very own Mount Zion — you actually lived here
        once!
    Come and visit the site of disaster,
    see how they've wrecked the sanctuary.

While your people were at worship, your enemies barged in,
    brawling and scrawling graffiti.
    They set fire to the porch;
    axes swinging, they chopped up the woodwork,
    Beat down the doors with sledgehammers,
    then split them into kindling.
    They burned your holy place to the ground,
    violated the place of worship.
    They said to themselves, "We'll wipe them all out,"
    and burned down all the places of worship.

There's not a sign or symbol of God in sight,
    nor anyone to speak in his name,
    no one who knows what's going on.
    How long, God, will barbarians blaspheme,
    enemies curse and get by with it?

Why don't you do something? How long are you going
to sit there with your hands folded in your lap?
God is my King from the very start;
he works salvation in the womb of the earth.
With one blow you split the sea in two,
you made mincemeat of the dragon Tannin.
You lopped off the heads of Leviathan,
then served them up in a stew for the animals.
With your finger you opened up springs and creeks,
and dried up the wild floodwaters.
You own the day, you own the night;
you put stars and sun in place.
You laid out the four corners of earth,
shaped the seasons of summer and winter.

Mark and remember, G OD, all the enemy
taunts, each idiot desecration.
Don't throw your lambs to the wolves;
after all we've been through, don't forget us.
Remember your promises;
the city is in darkness, the countryside violent.
Don't leave the victims to rot in the street;
make them a choir that sings your praises.

On your feet, O God —
stand up for yourself!
Do you hear what they're saying about you,
all the vile obscenities?
Don't tune out their malicious filth,
the brawling invective that never lets up.

My wife is crazy. Insane crazy. Necessity-of-medication crazy. I
mean, she's not on any medication, but there have been multiple
suggestions of this as a viable option voiced by me, when she, for
instance, would tap me on the shoulder to look out the window

at the UFO that was hovering in the night sky. I mean, I like it. It's endearing how she thinks that Roswell, New Mexico, is in fact where "the aliens" really live. Perhaps it was just too many *X-Files* episodes in her formative years, but I've argued that it's chemical.

One time we were eating with a couple of friends at a restaurant when the waitstaff erupted into one of those lame birthday songs. These sudden occurrences drive me out of my mind. I've yet to meet anyone who enjoys these outbursts. No one wants to wear that stupid hat, and no free dessert is worthy of such volume subjected on the rest of the quietly eating public. I always hold my ears when the yelling and clapping starts. I would swear that pans were being beaten on this particular evening, and when we'd gathered ourselves after the initial shock of wondering what violence was about to commence and our minds had sorted through all possible disasters and landed on the appropriate conclusion of "oh, the lame birthday song," I noticed that in my wife's hand is her table knife. Granted it was completely dull and couldn't cut through the butter earlier, but the fact that with cat-like speed her first instinct was to reach for the nearest instrument of aggression is somewhat disconcerting. On this particular occasion she wasn't in her usual "gunfighter seat" as she calls it—back to a corner facing outward so she can see everyone's comings and goings and no one can "sneak up on her"—so she didn't have the view of the spontaneous party that we were afforded. I calmly took the knife from her hand, placed it back on the table, and explained to her that it was okay, just someone's birthday. Meanwhile I thought to myself, *This rules. My wife would wish to wreak havoc on the lame-song birthday singers. I completely love this woman.* But what I said out loud was, "Really, we should look into medical solutions for this."

Another example of the difference between the sane workings of my cerebral functions and the imbalances present in my wife's occurred about a year ago. It was dead-of-Texas-winter, and we found ourselves in Lubbock. The sky was snowing Texas snow. Texas snow is sloppy. It is not pretty and does not contain the category of snow-flakes little children cut out of white paper and hang in windows or from your tree or from classroom ceilings. It is a bit of H_2O, barely not liquid. It does not float or drift toward the ground gently like you see in the movies or Colorado or Canada. It is more pulled by the earth, like the ground just wants to get it out of the sky, as if it finds it unpleasing to behold and just wants to get it over with quickly rather than draw it out and cause us all such aesthetic suffering.

We were spending the night in a Holiday Inn. At one time this particular hotel had an indoor pool. A Holidome is what it would have been called in its days of glory. Now, as you may or may not be aware, in a Holidome all of the rooms face inside so your doors and windows look out into the technological wonder of indoor aquatics. I was very pleased to be here, as some of the best birthday parties I'd attended as a small child were in a Holidome extraordinarily similar to what this one had been in its prime.

That night, we got in bed and turned out the lights. There was a gap in the curtain. Light was finding its way in and the sliver of luminosity somehow fell directly across my face. I hate this. It is a short-sheeting of the curtains. I growl words and fling myself back out of bed and begin the overly animated process of trying to find an appropriate overlap technique that will hold through the night. Of course, there are several attempts that bait me back to the bed, only to have it release just as I settle. I make promises out loud that on all future travels, I will start bringing duct tape or a proper sewing kit with buttons and Velcro or that handheld stitching machine we saw on the infomercial the other night, as I cannot deal with such mockery as this. I tell my wife that *they* do this on purpose. They probably watch us struggle and thrash about in attempts to generate the correct surface friction to adhere and to span this gap, knowing it will take just enough time for them to get a good chuckle and that is all they desire. That's why they weave them out of this slick material. They know these curtains to be unbecoming, but ocular splendor is not their draping intent. It is the glossy, frictionless tactile features they're interested in and nothing more. After much effort and only small speckles of light intruding here and there, I fall into deepest sleep.

I awoke. It was dark. I did not know what time it was. It was blackest dark. I had never seen such dark. I lay there blinking. There wasn't light anywhere. I looked in every direction possible and there was nothing but black. I rubbed my eyes. I opened them. I couldn't tell if I had opened them, so I tried again. I felt my face. I moved my hand an inch away and stared with as much intensity as I could gather. Black. I lay there. My heart was beating way too fast. My breath was short. I couldn't believe it. I was blind. At some point in the night I had lost my sight. It was probably because I had gotten so upset about the curtains. It was because I had wished for darkness and now it had come. I would have darkness for the rest of my living days. I was trying to decide if I would use the stick or the dog and was weighing the advantages and disadvantages of each when I thought about my wife lying there next to me so peacefully unaware of my new condition. I should tell her. I lay there a few moments more. She would be sad. I finally found the courage to tap her and announce to her my sightless fate. "Toni." Nothing. I tapped again with less tranquil tone. "Toni."

She immediately gasped at the darkness, grabbed my arm and sat straight up in the bed and hauntingly whispered, "Oh, no! It's the end of the world!"

Relief flooded in. I was not blind.

Now she was screaming.

This was amazing. *I was not blind.*

She was now shrieking about bombs and how she had known the end was soon and something about Lawrence Welk and the Texas snow being connected to all of this.

"I am not blind!" I yelled back with emotive inflection.

In between her gasps I calmly asked her why, if indeed it were the end of the world, would we be floating through pitch-black eternity on a Holiday Inn mattress? If this is what has awaited us in the ever-after it is an extreme disappointment to say the least. She agreed and we tried to call the front desk.

As you readily see, she is insane and I am the levelheaded anchor in this relationship.

In this psalm, the lights go out. In this psalm, we have lost our orientation, and our heads jump ahead uncontrollably to possibilities that are as dark as the air surrounding us. It is a psalm of communal lament. The community of Israel is mourning the loss of their Zion. It is quite easy for us to resonate with psalms of personal lament or personal praise. We connect with these psalms because our life experience is understood on a personal, privatized level. We are culturally shaped in a way that makes it more difficult for us to attach to corporate experience. For the people of Israel, the loss of Jerusalem was as tragic a thing that could have pressed in on them. This psalm informs us that it is biblical to feel and process our public experiences. It may be more tedious than our private, personal processing, but it is appropriate. And it is something we have lost along the way.

Every room was dark that winter Lubbock night at the Holiday Inn, and there was something shared in the darkness. There was something gained in the sharing of our experiences. To pursue praise properly we will bring our public moments into this pursuit, and in doing so we may even gain perspective.

Walter Brueggemann writes about communal laments such as this:

[They] are statements about the religious dimension of public events of loss. They permit us to remember that we are indeed public citizens and creatures and have an immediate, direct, and personal stake in public events. The recovery of this mode of psalmic prayer may be important if we are to overcome our general religious abdication of public issues and the malaise of indifference and apathy that comes with the abdication.[22]

Our capacity to feel public loss was greatly expanded on September 11, 2001. Before those images burned into our minds most of us actually imagined a world no larger than the boundary of our skin. Everything else seemed some sort of nonreality. True praise exists in the public and the private, and true praise erupts from the public and the private. We are all in our rooms when the darkness falls, and we must make effort to come outside and look each other in the eyes, or if the night still covers and we cannot yet see, we must reach out our hands to feel the lines on each other's weathered faces and fumble to feel and trace our mouths as they speak words of shared understanding and longing. And in our embracing, sparks of praise will splinter the darkness like fireworks.

# PSALM 75

We thank you, God, we thank you —
    your Name is our favorite word;
    your mighty works are all we talk about.

You say, "I'm calling this meeting to order,
    I'm ready to set things right.
    When the earth goes topsy-turvy
    And nobody knows which end is up,
    I nail it all down,
    I put everything in place again.
    I say to the smart alecks, 'That's enough,'
    to the bullies, 'Not so fast.'"

Don't raise your fist against High God.
    Don't raise your voice against Rock of Ages.
    He's the One from east to west;
    from desert to mountains, he's the One.

God rules: he brings this one down to his knees,
    pulls that one up on her feet.
    GOD has a cup in his hand,
    a bowl of wine, full to the brim.
    He draws from it and pours;
    it's drained to the dregs.
    Earth's wicked ones drink it all,
    drink it down to the last bitter drop!

And I'm telling the story of God Eternal,
*   singing the praises of Jacob's God.*
The fists of the wicked
are bloody stumps,
The arms of the righteous
are lofty green branches.

I must tell you that my wife's capacity for caring is equal to or greater than her capacity for conspiracy and imagination. In fact, it's like no other. I'm repeatedly astounded by her selfless munificence and am often inspired to live in a different way because of the encountering of it.

I think it runs in her family. It's just in their blood. Her Aunt Sandra oozed generosity. It dripped from her. Several years ago we watched as Sandra, a mother of five daughters, went through surely as much difficulty as one person could bear. We continually begged God on her behalf, telling Him that no one could stand more, and then something new would detonate in her life, compounding and adding to her burdens. Throughout all of this she constantly extended this seemingly inherited generosity of spirit to those around her. On June 24, 1999, she lost her fight with breast cancer and died at the age of forty.

The summer after Sandra's leaving, Toni and I had carved out a week for a vacation. It was much needed and much looked forward to, as we had not had such a thing in a very long while. Three of Sandra's daughters were ages six (Jordan), seven (Caitlyn), and nine (Madison) that summer. Toni determined that it would make for a wonderful vacation, sure to be full of recuperation and relaxation, if we toted them along with us on our trip to Disney World. We do not have any children. This sounded a simple enough task that would still firmly retain enough speculative adventure to more than make up for the absence of past vacations. So we loaded up our Suburban, painted "Are We There Yet?!" and "Walt Disney World or Bust!" on the windows in shoe polish, and pointed the vehicle in a general Floridian direction.

The drive unfolded in a manner that was to be expected, barring only a few unforeseen miniature exceptions—three tiny girl bladders. There were more bathroom breaks than typical. We quickly learned that the ability for retaining forty-four-ounce Big Gulps is diminutive in children. And one morning we were informed by the oldest of the three that the new Britney Spears CD was "in stores" that day. We nodded agreeably and unrelentingly continued driving. We did not realize until Mississippi that this was as compulsory as the previous restroom breaks. Thirteen hours later I knew every word to every song.

Little girls are impossible to keep up with. They are like a mist. I can't keep track of inanimate objects, such as keys and wallets and mobile phones, much less living, breathing little girls. I have never slept so well as those nights after a day in the park. Toni, however, would with frequency wake up in the middle of the night to walk the room in order to count and make sure everyone was still there. She explained this feeling that woke her as similar to the sensation of lying in bed while your body still feels in perpetual motion from all of the rides ridden that day, only this was a feeling of perpetual head counting after a day of perpetual head counting, and she could not make it stop. We now understand those leashes that some parents use to tether their kids. Before that trip we had poked fun and talked in hushed tones of the cruelty of the leash.

The whole of the trip was a success in so many unquantifiable terms. Fun was had by all; that was certain. We saw Mickey and Minnie and Donald and "Tweedle Dumb and Tweedle Dumber," as Caitlyn referred to them to their face, and we rode every ride that they were tall enough to ride, and we ate in Cinderella's Castle, and we watched Tinkerbell fly into the night, and we saw the light parade with that cool Moog music that seemed generated by the night air or maybe from inside you (it was too hard to tell), and we got sunburns by the pool with real sand in the bottom of it, and we ate pancakes in the shape of Mickey and couldn't decide if this was good or bad to eat such a kind mouse and had meaningful conversations coming to a decisive conclusion that if you must in fact eat Mickey you should start at his ear as it will be less painful for him and he will know what's coming and it will give him time to prepare, and we waited for Alice from Wonderland to come to our table so we could ask her if they had pancakes in the shape of her because she was starting to bug us, and we held hands, five of us across, to see if people would walk around us or try to bust through, and for the most part there were no real outbursts of anger or verbal abuse—until the very end of our return trip, a mere thirty miles from home. As Britney apologized for doing it again, Toni turned and spied conspiracy in the quietness of the Suburban's backseat that sent her into rage. Now, one thing we had learned is that whenever there is quiet and three little girls occupying the same time and space, something is not right.

While walking out of the park down Main Street, Disney, for the last time, headed for the monorail and our return to childlessness, the girls had pleaded with little-girl pleading for suckers the size of their heads that they had spotted in the doorway of the last corner shop. Here is a diagram of proportion comparison of these suckers to the average-size seven-year-old cranium.

a. sucker   b. seven-year-old cranium

Of course we explained that we were just going to get in the Suburban and head straight for home and that they "cannot eat the sucker in the car," as we had learned by now that most food will end up all over whatever is in close proximity to consumption. This was nonnegotiable. And so it was agreed upon by all that no suckers would be eaten in the vehicle. Now, thirty minutes from home, Caitlyn's tongue and sucker had met and Toni had spied the surreptitious slurp. So my wife, with loud volume, demands the sucker be passed up front to her. Sucker in hand, she discovers that the price tag has been peeled back and a tiny hole underneath it reveals a small tongue-sized cavity. This craftiness had been happening for who knows how long and I, amused by such artful wiliness, began laughing. This did not help matters, and before any of us knew what was going on, the window was down and the sucker was flying, Frisbee-like, away from us all. I could not believe it! How could she? Now the three girls were crying.

"Why did you throw-ow Caitlyn's sucker-er (sniff) out the window-ow-ow?" Madison begged through choking tears.

My wife calmly asked, "Did I tell her not to eat the sucker?"

"Yeeessss," came the tearful unison response from the trio in the back.

"Did you tell me you would not?"

"Yeeessss."

"There are consequences to your actions and disobedience."

I was in awe. This woman's wisdom was infectious. I did, however, point out to her and her cousins that Toni had littered and they should not do this either as there would be consequences for her actions and disobedience. Then came the first violence of the trip as she hit me in the arm.

I love it that Psalm 75 follows Psalm 74. I don't revel exclusively in the numeric ordering necessarily, although I do find it agreeable on an organizational level, but I do think it incredibly appropriate that the subject matter flows in such a way. Psalm 74 starts, "You walked off and left us," and then we have Psalm 75 beginning, "We thank you, God, we thank you." It's beautiful, really, for such disparities to exist so close to one another. But the real gem I think in Psalm 75 is the simple proverbial instructions of it. "Don't raise your fist against High God. Don't raise your voice against Rock of Ages." There is simple wisdom here. There are consequences for wrongs. Even when we have been covered by grace, when we have been met with a gift that exceeds imagination and is beyond every hope, when the kingdom of heaven is underfoot, there still is a choosing and consequences that come as a direct result of that choosing.

PSALM 84

What a beautiful home, GOD of the Angel Armies!
  I've always longed to live in a place like this,
  Always dreamed of a room in your house,
  where I could sing for joy to God-alive!

Birds find nooks and crannies in your house,
  sparrows and swallows make nests there.
  They lay their eggs and raise their young,
  singing their songs in the place where we worship.
  GOD of the Angel Armies! King! God!
  How blessed they are to live and sing there!

And how blessed all those in whom you live,
  whose lives become roads you travel;
  They wind through lonesome valleys, come upon
      brooks,
  discover cool springs and pools brimming with rain!
  God-traveled, these roads curve up the mountain, and
  at the last turn — Zion! God in full view!

God of the Angel Armies, listen:
  O God of Jacob, open your ears — I'm praying!
  Look at our shields, glistening in the sun,
  our faces, shining with your gracious anointing.

One day spent in your house, this beautiful place of
worship,
  beats thousands spent on Greek island beaches.

*I'd rather scrub floors in the house of my God
than be honored as a guest in the palace of sin.
All sunshine and sovereign is GOD,
generous in gifts and glory.
He doesn't scrimp with his traveling companions.
It's smooth sailing all the way with GOD of the Angel
Armies.*

I don't like public restrooms. I hate the whole idea of waste and its disposal. I've spent quite a bit of time wondering if waste, as a by-product of our consumption, was something intended from the beginning. There is nothing glamorous or redeemable about it as far as I can tell, and I can't imagine a place called "paradise" having to deal with the problems of waste removal. Surely, in the "new creation" of things this will not be overlooked.

So you can imagine my disdain for public restrooms. Automated public restrooms make me especially nervous. Automatic toilets, automatic sinks, automatic soap dispensers, and automatic towel or blow-dry technologies are now commonplace. These things make me anxious. So much so that I try to avoid at all costs a trip to the little cowboys' room while in a public place. Most folks avoid public facilities because they're "public" in access and typically not preserved in pristine state, but me, I steer clear because I'm afraid of an encounter with something of the optical automatic eye variety. See, my experience is that I will walk in, address the urinal, be standing there doing what is necessary, thinking myself to be fully present, when all of a sudden the urinal I'm standing in front of flushes. It always flushes *while I'm still there.* And immediately all these existential metaphysical thoughts and questions of existence, or lack thereof, go careening through my head: *I'm here. I know I'm here. I am certain I am here. Or am I? It flushed. If I were here, it would not have flushed. Would it? Perhaps I'm here but it doesn't know I'm here? Or maybe it's not here?* All of these questions are more than my feeble mind can stand, so my defense mechanism is avoidance. But when there is no choice, when all other options or straining muscles have been exhausted and I must enter into the domain of the optical automatic eye, I have developed two approaches:

Approach A — Constant Movement

I approach the urinal in overly exaggerated action and then remain in motion throughout the necessary process. This may include a rocking of my weight from one foot to the other in a side-to-side action or marching in place — not a high-knee forward march, as that would become awkward, but a march with the feet only lifted perhaps three-and-a-half inches off the ground and the knees raising to the side in a bowlegged manner or, if the urinal is at a level low enough, I will squat/stand, squat/stand, squat/stand — again, not an overly exaggerated squat all the way to the ground, just a lowering of my body by a few inches just sufficient for the watchful toilet eye to see that I am here. And as I am thinking nervous thoughts — constant movement, constant movement — and holding my breath — side-to-side, side-to-side — and as I am glancing around the restroom to nod and smile at my fellow man in assurance that everything is okay — squat/stand, squat/stand — as I am fully aware of the ludicrous nature of my appearance and hope to divert their obvious thoughts of madness with my projected reassuring nonverbals — keep moving, keep moving — and then . . . *flush* . . . It always flushes. And the questions come in a spraying torrent, and my mind is again unsettled and crowded.

Approach B — Covert Inanimateness

I approach stealthily, every movement under-the-radar, slow and fluid. You would never see me coming. Once

I am in position, I stand perfectly still. I am barely breathing. My nerves are asleep. I am motionless. This approach does not bring upon you nearly the amount of attention as Approach A, so there is no need to project constant assurances of sanity about the room. I am free to fully engage in my impassive concentration. I lock eyes with the sensor, unafraid as I know it is the fear they feed on. Do Not Move! Do Not Move! Do Not Move! . . . *flush* . . . It always flushes. There is mockery in this flush as the eye stares back unflinching. And my mind is again a disconcerted liquid of questioning.

I hate public restrooms.

There aren't many places I'd rather not be than a public restroom and especially one with automatic conveniences. Yet Psalm 84 sends us there, or in the very least it lets us know it is an option.

Psalm 84 is often romanticized. We read a line that goes something like, "One day with You is better than a thousand anywhere else," and we think of lovers lost in each other's eyes, floating in embrace, a million miles from anywhere. What a line. It would melt you to have that whispered in the ear. But the context that follows totally ruins it.

There are two options here. For option A, imagine yourself a houseguest. "Please come in. Make yourself at home. What's mine is yours. Can I get you anything? Here is your bed; it is made with our best linens. We only get these out when folks like you come over. The table is set with our best silver. We have cooked all day. Please sit down. Take your shoes off. *Mi casa es su casa.*" Or option B, "Here is a pail of water and a scrub brush. You'll need to put a lot of muscle into it, as the dirt has been here a great length of time. You might need to use bleach and let it set for just a bit. Mind that you don't get it on you, as it will eat through your garments or cause them to turn a yellowish white."

It sounds much less romantic to think that the rest of the declaration could be, "I understand that to be with you may in fact mean degradation rather than accommodation."

We have not been promised palatial housing, but we have been promised His presence. We often find ourselves in spaces that seem the last spot on earth we would have picked to insert ourselves, engaged in things that we never imagined ourselves having to do, but we can know this comfort: that wherever we are, we are in the very residence of God and this is sweeter and greater than anywhere without Him. We carry His residence into these spaces. Perhaps we're on our hands and knees with sponge and soap because someone has just made a mess of things or maybe we've just noticed that most places we inhabit are in need of cleaning. Living praise often leads us close to the ground. To dirt. It often leads to industry that is unglamorous and unromantic. It often leads us to sweat and toil and lonesome valleys. But around the bend are cool springs. These moments are holy because we know that wherever we find ourselves we are in the very house of God. And there is space and comfort here exceeding anything offered elsewhere. Even if it leads us to dark places on our hands and knees, it is sweeter than lying on a beach in Greece because the sunshine of our Maker's presence is brighter and stronger than a thousand stars, and it reaches to wherever we are.

"You Are Here"

"Look, Dave, I can see you're really upset about this. . . . "
(2001: A Space Odyssey)

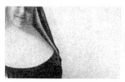

PSALM 88

GOD, you're my last chance of the day.
   I spend the night on my knees before you.
   Put me on your salvation agenda;
   take notes on the trouble I'm in.
   I've had my fill of trouble;
   I'm camped on the edge of hell.
   I'm written off as a lost cause,
   one more statistic, a hopeless case.
   Abandoned as already dead,
   one more body in a stack of corpses,
   And not so much as a gravestone —
   I'm a black hole in oblivion.
   You've dropped me into a bottomless pit,
   sunk me in a pitch-black abyss.
   I'm battered senseless by your rage,
   relentlessly pounded by your waves of anger.
   You turned my friends against me,
   made me horrible to them.
   I'm caught in a maze and can't find my way out,
   blinded by tears of pain and frustration.

I call to you, GOD; all day I call.
   I wring my hands, I plead for help.
   Are the dead a live audience for your miracles?
   Do ghosts ever join the choirs that praise you?
   Does your love make any difference in a graveyard?
   Is your faithful presence noticed in the corridors of
      hell?

Are your marvelous wonders ever seen in the dark,
your righteous ways noticed in the Land of No
    Memory?

I'm standing my ground, GOD, shouting for help,
    at my prayers every morning, on my knees each
        daybreak.
Why, GOD, do you turn a deaf ear?
Why do you make yourself scarce?
For as long as I remember I've been hurting;
I've taken the worst you can hand out, and I've had it.
Your wildfire anger has blazed through my life;
I'm bleeding, black and blue.
You've attacked me fiercely from every side,
raining down blows till I'm nearly dead.
You made lover and neighbor alike dump me;
the only friend I have left is Darkness.

I have a recent fascination with pinhole cameras. I'm not a photographer. I don't even like photographers much (except you there who might be reading this, but you're the only one). I get nervous when those cute tourist couples ask me, a passerby, to stop and take their picture. All the buttons and verbal instructions shouted from these strangers that have no right to talk that loudly to you: "You've got to hold it down for five seconds!" "No, the other button!" "Can you get the bird as it flies by in the background?!" "Your finger is blocking the lens!" And all of this shouted as if the camera has robbed me of my hearing. I hear fine. I've got excellent hearing but I'm no photographer. Pinhole cameras, though, are almost comically primitive. Typically homemade, they lack lenses, traditional shutters, light meters, and focusing controls. They're nothing more than a little box with a pinhole in it. Exposing a sheet of film placed inside may require thirty seconds, a couple of minutes, or all day. There's no viewfinder, so to quote an overdramatic friend of mine, "You must relinquish your soul to the camera." Photographers.

Consider this: The daylight illuminating the wall of a room actually forms a jumble of overlapping images from that which is outside the window as light bounces off these objects. The light on the wall is, in fact, an upside-down projection of the scene outside your window, just a very, very, very fuzzy one. Shrink the window dramatically, and the room works like a pinhole camera, sharpening (yet dimming) the upside-down image on the wall. When the opening admits only a single faint cone of daylight into the darkened room, it negates the confusion of overlapping light rays and makes things come into focus. You could, if you were a photographer, capture this image with a more traditional lens camera by leaving the shutter open for a long time, depending on how sharp you wanted the image. Photographs taken in this manner just blow my mind.

"When images of illuminated objects . . . penetrate through a small hole into a very dark room . . . you will see [on the opposite wall] these objects in their proper form and color, reduced in size . . . in a reversed position, owing to the intersection of the rays." Leonardo da Vinci

I love most the idea that images are entering your space without your intending it. We build a room to keep the outside, outside and the inside, inside—and we fail. Without asking, the outside comes in through the tiniest of holes and imposes itself on us in our protected areas.

Psalm 88 is this. A picture of a moment when life has pressed in and faith is turned on its head and the writer has been thrown into a deluge with the overpowering weight of the moment. Life cannot be kept at bay. It comes. Our protected areas are invaded. We cry for help and hear silence in return. I think the truth in this chapter is that sometimes we find ourselves overwhelmed with no answer. In this psalm there are no reasons given for God's silence. The psalm is not interested in explanation. We may imagine that the situation is so desperate that even if a "reason" could be offered, the speaker would have no interest in it, nor would it help, because the needfulness of the moment supersedes any reasonable conversation. But the psalmist was not deterred by the silence. Even if the speaker is speaking to the empty sky, he is not deterred. It only leads to more intense address. This psalm reports what it's like to be God's partner in His inexplicable absence. There is nothing out of bounds, nothing precluded or inappropriate. Everything properly belongs in this conversation of the heart. To withhold parts of life from that conversation is to withhold parts of life from the sovereignty of God. God must be addressed even if God never answers. In our modern experience it is believed that enough power and knowledge can tame the terror and eliminate the darkness. But we regularly learn and discern that there in the darkness—more than anywhere else—newness that is not of our own making breaks upon us and we are surely then drowned in Him. Psalm 88 shows us what the cross is about: faithfulness in scenes of complete abandonment.[23]

PSALM 96

Sing GOD a brand-new song!
 Earth and everyone in it, sing!
 Sing to GOD — worship GOD!

Shout the news of his victory from sea to sea,
 Take the news of his glory to the lost,
 News of his wonders to one and all!

For GOD is great, and worth a thousand Hallelujahs.
 His terrible beauty makes the gods look cheap;
 Pagan gods are mere tatters and rags.

GOD made the heavens —
 Royal splendor radiates from him,
 A powerful beauty sets him apart.

Bravo, GOD, Bravo!
 Everyone join in the great shout: Encore!
 In awe before the beauty, in awe before the might.

Bring gifts and celebrate,
 Bow before the beauty of GOD,
 Then to your knees — everyone worship!

Get out the message — GOD Rules!
 He put the world on a firm foundation;
 He treats everyone fair and square.

Let's hear it from Sky,
With Earth joining in,
And a huge round of applause from Sea.

Let Wilderness turn cartwheels,
Animals, come dance,
Put every tree of the forest in the choir —

An extravaganza before GOD as he comes,
As he comes to set everything right on earth,
Set everything right, treat everyone fair.

One thing I wanted desperately as a child was a nickname. I would spend afternoons writing potential nicknames on pieces of paper until I found one I thought fitting and then I'd prance around the house announcing to everyone that I would no longer be answering to "David." "From now on I will only respond to 'Speedy'" or some other equally veritable definitude. Yet nothing would stick and I would become terribly sad. My dad would yell from the other room, "David, it's time for dinner." I would respond, "David no longer answers to 'David' but 'Tiger,' remember?" To which he would reply, "David Wallace Crowder, you get in here right now!" And of course I'd oblige.

My great uncle Thelen had a John Deere tractor. When I close my eyes I can smell the diesel fuel and his aftershave. He would let me sit on his knee and ride with him. One afternoon he let me take the wheel, and as I was deftly assisting him in making another turn, he stated, "DW, you're a natural."

"What?" I asked.

"I said, 'DW, you are a natural.'"

"Why did you call me DW?" I said almost breathless, comprehending the full weight of potential in this statement.

"Because that's my nickname for you."

I was floating. "Oh. Yeah, but why DW?" I asked.

"It's your initials."

"What about Rascal, or Tex, or Cowboy?"

"Nope. You're a DW if ever there was one."

So I had a nickname. I began to tell everyone to call me DW — I *was* DW — but alas, it still wouldn't stick. Except for Uncle Thelen. I never again heard him call me David, and I loved him for it.

In Old Testament times, names were significant. They held identity as well as identification. In this psalm we encounter the only "proper" name given for God: Yahweh. In *The Message*, "GOD" (small-capped) designates the word *Yahweh*. It appears nine times in Psalm 96, which is quite frequent considering the brevity of this psalm. The name "Yahweh" — or the tetragrammaton, *YHWH* — is the one revealed to Moses at the burning bush, and in most Christian translations of the Bible, it appears as "LORD." The Jewish community substituted "LORD" for this proper name for fear of speaking His name in vain. They felt unworthy to utter such a name. It is anything but empty of meaning. It specifies immediacy, a presence: the verb form "to be," which in Mosaic context is a "being present."[24] The meaning can best be summarized as "present to act, (usually but not only) in salvation."[25] Do you see the beauty here? It's unbelievable. The defining attribute, the identity of God, is "present rescuer." His name holds for us the very promise of presence. It is who He is. He is here. He is in the middle of the stuff we are in the middle of. No wonder trees break into song here. No wonder encores are called for. It is Yahweh. Our Deliverer, our Salvation, our Promise is here; He is here and we must sing and shout and bow down and clap and roar and applaud and dance; dance, everyone, dance and fall to your knees.

This is a name that sticks. This is a name that defines. This is a name that in its very utterance births life. Our God is present. He comes to set things right. In His very name is rescue. This is who He is. There is not a moment in human history that has eluded His gaze. There is not a second in your life that He was not around. He is unavoidable. He is inescapable. He is inevitable and undeniable. He is.

 PSALM 100

On your feet now — applaud GOD!
 Bring a gift of laughter,
  sing yourselves into his presence.

Know this: GOD is God, and God, GOD.
 He made us; we didn't make him.
  We're his people, his well-tended sheep.

Enter with the password: "Thank you!"
 Make yourselves at home, talking praise.
  Thank him. Worship him.

For GOD is sheer beauty,
 all-generous in love,
  loyal always and ever.

My parents are amazing people, devout in their faith and intent on bringing my brother and me up in a godly manner. Their parenting was brilliant, really. There were unexpected lessons hidden at every turn. But I, like most children, raised issue every once in a while regarding the rule and reign of the sovereign Crowder territory. One thing that I found rather disturbing was my parents' purchase and use of generic food. I'm unsure of the reasoning behind this generic food acquisition, whether it was simply leftover sensitivities to Cold War stockpiling, whose grip had become too tenacious to shake, or if it was just frugalness. The Cold War thing made some sense due to the fact that we had white bags on white bags of instant mashed potatoes with the black New Times Roman font indicating their government genesis and hoards of cheese coming from the same said government. Perhaps the government cheese was actually issued during the Cold War and my father had simply frozen it all so it would keep. This seemed somewhat logical, seeing as we constantly had a freezer full of frozen milk. It computed that perhaps this is what you are to do with dairy. (Although I'm not at all sure if the government cheese could truly be categorized in the dairy family. It is the one and only cheese I have encountered that disintegrates into a crumbling, dirt-like texture when cut or chewed. It has since been my observation that cheeses, for the most part, tend *not* to be dusty powder in their consistency.)

But the question loomed as to where the cheese came from. I knew my dad did not work for the government. At least I didn't think so, which led me to believe for a very long time that he was a spy. This made sense. He was a spy, and so that is why the milk was frozen and thawed one carton at a time, because he had inside information that milk would never again be stickered with a price tag marked $1.10. With this espionage knowledge, I could then function within our culinary boundaries and even feel a clever sense of joy while trying to make a cheese sandwich out of yellow-orange dust. I would smile as it was coating my choking lips and as I coughed clouds of covert cheese.

I was well into high school before I began to question out loud our dietary sources. I'd gently inquire such things as, "So, when do you think we'll run out of the frozen milk?" or "Has anyone noticed that water has a lower melting point than the rest of the white stuff in the carton? It sure gets a lot thicker toward the end, huh?" or "So you, like, saved a nickel, huh? Wow. Multiply that times the 180 cartons you got, times most of my bowls of cereal, and that equals a lot, huh?"

But the biggest conflicts were over the cereal itself. I tell you now that generic cereal is a bad thing. There is no amount of money saved that can make Sugar Flakes taste good when it is the Frosted Flake your tongue craves. They are not equals. It is appalling to think of, but for a nickel or two less you can purchase a thing such as Fruit Hoops in substitution of Fruit Loops. There should be state regulation of this. My father and I would go around and around on this point of contention. Yes, they look the same. Yes, the names sound similar. But no, they do not taste anywhere near the same food group. I would tell my father things like, "Dad, it has the smell and taste of roast beef. This is not pleasing to me at 7:00 a.m." And he would respond, "Son, the Fruit Hoop is just as tasty as the Fruit Loop. You could not separate them in a blind taste test." I would then mumble that he drank too many hot liquids as a child and would just as soon eat chalk as a steak, with a motto like "It all goes to the same place" touted at every meal. It came to the point where my father finally bowed—just a little; he purchased a genuine box of Fruit Loops with *the* Toucan Sam on the front and everything. There were even real prizes in the bottom of the box. But without our knowledge, when the box was getting low, when we had taken in most of the goodness that it once held, my father filled it up with Fruit Hoops. Inconceivable! He put Fruit Hoops in the box of Fruit Loops to prove to us that there is no discernable difference between the two tastes. Immediately, the morning of the heist, I spit out what I had just so joyously delivered to my mouth, something most certainly and surprisingly of the meat-flavored variety. "DAD!"

Here in this psalm we are reminded that there is only one true Yahweh God. Hear His name again. Yahweh. There is only one ever-present Maker; there is only one Center. Oh, sure, there is constant competition for His replacement, but it is just impossible. All the little gods at whose feet we place our affections don't even have it in them to be ever-present. Yahweh God doesn't have it in Him to *not* be present. He can't. It would defy who He is to be anywhere but here and now, wherever that may be. There is no substitute that will taste right. Everything else is just a choking powder, a mist, a vapor, a melting, watered-down attempt at displacement. We did not create this God. We did not dream Him up. There is no dream or imagination that could contain Him. He is beyond dreaming. Let your mind wander, let it stretch to bounds it hasn't dared before, in search of an end to this God, and you will find only spaces more vast and wide and open than your eyes and heart can take in. There is no end, I tell you. There is no beginning even. And we have lived for temporal pleasures, for but a moment here and there, we have grasped for things near and attainable, we have ingested what was illusory fulfillment, and I beg you now to spit it out. It is of the wrong flavor. It is breakfast cereal that tastes of roast beef and is only edible because we have the wrong ideas about what is good. There is no substitute for The Ever-Present God of gods. He is complete beauty. Stare into the most faithful of loves until He is burned into your retinas, until everywhere you look He is superimposed upon the landscape.

 # PSALM 113

Hallelujah!
>*You who serve GOD, praise GOD!*
>*Just to speak his name is praise!*
>*Just to remember GOD is a blessing —*
>*now and tomorrow and always.*
>*From east to west, from dawn to dusk,*
>*keep lifting all your praises to GOD!*

GOD is higher than anything and anyone,
>*outshining everything you can see in the skies.*
>*Who can compare with GOD, our God,*
>*so majestically enthroned,*
>*Surveying his magnificent*
>*heavens and earth?*
>*He picks up the poor from out of the dirt,*
>*rescues the wretched who've been thrown out with the*
>>*trash,*
>*Seats them among the honored guests,*
>*a place of honor among the brightest and best.*
>*He gives childless couples a family,*
>*gives them joy as the parents of children.*
>*Hallelujah!*

I have a question. What contains sugar, corn syrup, gelatin, and less than .5 percent of the following: potassium sorbate, artificial flavors, yellow no. 5, carnauba wax?

Or, to be more specific, what is $C_{12}H_{22}O_{11}$, gelatin, and $C_{16}H_9N_4NA_3O_9S_2$?

I refer you again to appendix D.

My friend Mike, who is smarter than the rest of us (yes, including you), said it was a good thing I didn't want to write out the chemical formula for shampoo. I asked why and he said, "It would fill up two pages."

"Why?"

"'Cause shampoo has long molecules. It's freaky."

"All shampoo?"

"Yeah. It just has weird big molecules. This is a bizarre conversation."

"What about, like, Head & Shoulders?"

"Yeah. Freaky long. Pyrithione zinc. It's in your standard Selsun Blue, Head & Shoulders, et cetera. This feels like an interrogation."

"So, like the pyrithione zinc gets rid of the dandruff?"

"Sort of. You wouldn't understand. Now leave me alone so I can read my C++ manual."

Here is what I do know: If you removed yellow no. 5 from the previously mentioned merger of elements you wouldn't have a cuddly little yellow Peep, you'd have a scary white chicken. Take out the sugar and you just have a foul-flavored gelatin, and I don't want to tell you what gelatin is made of.[26]

Here's the thing: the main ingredient when it comes to God is GOD. Divinity. There is no imitation. There is no Splenda substitute. If you haven't noticed yet this is a trend in the Psalms. There is only one God. He is not like us. He is wholly transcendent. His condition is not like ours. Yet here we find Him right in the middle of our plight and *this* is the miracle. This is what is incomprehensible. There is no amount of concentration that will help get your head around this. If you put life together in any way that doesn't include Yahweh Caps Lock GOD . . . it is not life.

First, God. God is the subject of life. God is foundational for living. If we don't have a sense of the primacy of God, we will never get it right, get life right, get *our* lives right. Not God at the margins; not God as an option; not God on the weekends. God at center and circumference; God first and last; God, God, God.

— EUGENE PETERSON [27]

PSALM 121

I look up to the mountains;
*   does my strength come from mountains?*
*   No, my strength comes from GOD,*
*   who made heaven and earth, and mountains.*

He won't let you stumble,
*   your Guardian God won't fall asleep.*
*   Not on your life! Israel's*
*   Guardian will never doze or sleep.*

GOD's your Guardian,
*   right at your side to protect you —*
*   Shielding you from sunstroke,*
*   sheltering you from moonstroke.*

GOD guards you from every evil,
*   he guards your very life.*
*   He guards you when you leave and when you return,*
*   he guards you now, he guards you always.*

Stretch Armstrong

"S-t-r-e-t-c-h him and he returns to normal size!"

In 1976 Kenner had one of the truly brilliant ideas in the history of Superhero Conception. Can you imagine the research and development meeting?:

"Okay, here's the concept: a new superhero that is made of some space-age material that we must invent that will allow his limbs to be pulled with great effort by small children, stretching him to four times his regular size, and then he'll snap right back in place!"

The devil's advocate inquires, "So his power is . . . you can pull his limbs?"

"Yes," responds the guy whose fault this is. "And he will have accessories. Did I mention the accessories? Oh, sorry, yes, he will have accessories, like a pair of shorts! Oh, and a Stretch-O-Graph!" And then in an existential fit of continuing brilliance, he adds, "And we should also make a stretching Pink Octopus, a Monster, and a see-thru Alien with X-ray vision!"

And Kenner did this. They heard this idea and nodded agreeably. They stood from the table shaking hands and patting backs with the congratulatorial ruffling of the idea-dreamer's hair. They made and marketed a mostly naked man whose appendages you were commanded to pull.

It was genius. All of my friends had one. We tortured Stretch daily. Who is capable of resisting a challenge from one whose very existence cries out for his attempted destruction and whose defiant promise is that it can't be done? Genius, I tell you! I mean, Superman was cool but as a kid you had no chance against such impenetrable strength. If he could pick up trains and get hit by bullets and stuff, there was certainly no harm that you, as a seven-year-old, could rain down upon him. Who can afford to travel into

space on penny allowances to gather that green stuff that was his only weakness?

Here Stretch led you on. You would pull and make progress. You felt like you were getting somewhere with this guy. And sure, he would return to his initial shape prior to your exertions, but there was no "snapping" back into place as promised on the package. No, his arms would lie there draping for a while. Then, slowly, he appeared to shrink back into original form. For a few postbicentennial summers, we spent long afternoons testing the endurance of Stretch and his enemies—until the limbs started to harden or get small cracks in them, causing this dark purple, miracle stretch-enabling goop to leak out. One of my friends rubbed this leaking liquid gelatin on his arm and told us to pull. Its powers were not transferable.

As children, we dreamed of heroes whose powers could not be thwarted, whose justice would be unavoidable, whose rescues were sure and strong. As we mature we gradually learn that each of these mythic heroes we loved and imagined real and present were mere figments, flawed with Achillean nonexistence or cracking plastics. We learn early as children that there is evil in the world and that we have a need for some external intervention because we are powerless.

This psalm is a reminder that our dreamings are not unfounded. This is the song of our Protector. Our Hero. Everything else falls apart. Every other savior is tragically blemished, and time will divulge innate inadequacies. Oh, the places and things we put our hopes in might hold together for a bit, but in the end they are but smoke and mirrors. In hindsight they are simple things that can be pulled apart by children. But not Yahweh. He is your Rescuer and your Protector. He doesn't deteriorate. His arms stretched the heavens and are still long enough to cover you wherever you may be. He is your constant Guardian. This is beyond everything you ever dreamed. This is grander than any intervention you concocted and portrayed as you flew your favorite hero into your childish plot. Yahweh GOD guards your very life. "He guards you now, he guards you always."

# PSALM 136

Thank GOD! He deserves your thanks.
    His love never quits.
    Thank the God of all gods,
    His love never quits.
    Thank the Lord of all lords.
    His love never quits.

Thank the miracle-working God,
    His love never quits.
    The God whose skill formed the cosmos,
    His love never quits.
    The God who laid out earth on ocean foundations,
    His love never quits.
    The God who filled the skies with light,
    His love never quits.
    The sun to watch over the day,
    His love never quits.
    Moon and stars as guardians of the night,
    His love never quits.
    The God who struck down the Egyptian firstborn,
    His love never quits.
    And rescued Israel from Egypt's oppression,
    His love never quits.
    Took Israel in hand with his powerful hand,
    His love never quits.
    Split the Red Sea right in half,
    His love never quits.
    Led Israel right through the middle,

His love never quits.
Dumped Pharaoh and his army in the sea,
His love never quits.
The God who marched his people through the desert,
His love never quits.
Smashed huge kingdoms right and left,
His love never quits.
Struck down the famous kings,
His love never quits.
Struck Sihon the Amorite king,
His love never quits.
Struck Og the Bashanite king,
His love never quits.
Then distributed their land as booty,
His love never quits.
Handed the land over to Israel.
His love never quits.

God remembered us when we were down,
His love never quits.
Rescued us from the trampling boot,
His love never quits.
Takes care of everyone in time of need.
His love never quits.
Thank God, who did it all!
His love never quits!

The neighborhood.

We moved when I was seven from Cooper Lane to a street by the name of Sleepy Hollow. I knew this was not a good thing, because I had read the legend and was convinced this street was indeed the one from these pages, although in the relating of this concern to my parents, I kept referring to Ebenezer Scrooge and getting all the details mucked up. The changing of neighborhoods can be a traumatic occurrence for children. I was terrified and saddened to be leaving the comfort of my Cooper Lane playmates. I was convinced and certain that nothing good could come of this relocation. There were woods behind this new house. Dark woods. On one of the contemplative visits with the Realtor, I stealthily snuck off to explore these woodlands while the adults walked and talked in the hallways of the Sleepy Hollow house. I heard voices and followed them. I found a tree house with three boys about my age in it. One of them introduced himself as Stephen Sullivan and told me he was a ninja. I thought these were the coolest kids I had ever seen ever. We bonded, became friends, and eventually went on to pull three Stretch Armstrongs apart.

Now, like any good American neighborhood we had a bully. Ours was named Sid. I'm talking the textbook caricature, lunch-money-stealing, beat-you-up kind. For real. He would steal all of the kids' lunch money and called it a toll for using his street and breathing his air. He was twenty years old in the second grade and eight times the size of any of the rest of us. I asked Stephen Sullivan about the ninja thing, if he could unload some of that ninja hurt on Sid, and he launched into an exposition explaining that ninjas were really a peaceful people and not prone to resort to violence unless there was no other course of action and held strong beliefs regarding nonviolent protest, and he then began to complain about how the ninjas were really a misrepresented people in movies and on television and this gave explanation for my confusion concerning his nonaggressive actions.

Now what I am about to relate to you, I do so in full knowledge of the risk that you may think much ill of me. But, alas, it is necessary.

After one particular trip around our block and after having been pulled from my miniature red bike (it had solid black rubber tires and was half the appropriate size for me, as I had recently hit a growth spurt) and after being pummeled and told things by Sid that I already knew, like, "Your bike has solid black rubber tires! It's half the appropriate size for you! Ha, ha, ha, ha, ha," I decided I would rescue the neighborhood. It had to be done. I thought of the children. There must be justice. There must be freedom. These streets were ours, and there would be no more tolls. This is our air, too, and we will breathe it free of charge.

I planned for weeks. The day came, and when the bell rang I ran from the classroom. I had ridden my bike that day, as I needed the speed. I road swiftly, hunched with knees deftly circumventing the handlebars. I threw the bike in the garage. I grabbed my BB gun that was hidden behind the trash can and ran. Sid lived two doors down. He had large juniper trees flanking the entrance to his front door. I hid behind the one on the right and waited breathlessly. I was shaking. I had practiced rapid, repetitious firing for weeks. I rehearsed my aim and the announcement of my presence. And I knew that what was about to be done had to be done decisively and without hesitation. I had lain in bed imagining what this moment would feel like, but I was unprepared. I couldn't control my legs. They were tremors of tissue. I was crying. Then I heard him. His feet were on the sidewalk. I could hear him sniffing. He was always sniffing because his nose ran constantly. He was at his door. I sprang from the juniper yelling, "FREEDOM!" and other things that made no sense. I shot him in the stomach and reloaded in the same instance. I shot again, this time in the leg, and my finely trained instinct already had another BB in the chamber. I shot again. He was on the ground in a ball and was crying, and I shot again and again. Now, this same gun had shot me on numerous occasions, as one of our favorite things to do in the woods was to have BB gun wars. We had been warned of the putting out of eyes and such, but we thought none of us a good enough shot to actually hit someone in the eye, and I will tell you that it doesn't hurt as bad as the portrayed pain unfolding at my feet. Sid was a wimp. I told him that this vehement act was for all the children of the neighborhood—that we would, from this day forth, walk the streets freely. That there were no more tolls to pay. That he would have to eat the lunch that his mother had packed and not my Twinkies or any other kids' Twinkies. That I would be behind every bush and every tree waiting for him to walk by, unsuspecting, if things did not end here. And most significantly, that I would tell everyone, *everyone,* how he had cried like a diminutive baby if he ever raised a hand against anyone again.

The next day Sid taught me Pig Latin in my driveway.

I am not proud of this horrific retribution and have told only the closest of friends about this aggressive act. I was young and had yet to learn the ways of Martin Luther King Jr. or comprehend the beauty of the ninja's nonviolence.

Toward the close of World War II, our fathers and grandfathers spent their existential apprenticeships in the readings of Kafka, Sartre's *La Nausee,* Camus's *L'Etranger.* These writings put philosophy in words and stories that brought it near and articulated the solitude, slavery, and freedom that were their experience. The anguish that they experienced and saw in the world was given a name and made more understandable. And in their endless philosophical discussions and conversations they rebuilt the world—richer, more just, happier—where the pursuit of happiness was more than some vague constitutional right or notion. They lived in historic moments that made this necessity more present and desperate. They lived with fear of holocaust because they had seen one. They knew the evils we were capable of because they were written in their newspapers and blinking on their televisions and buried in their graveyards, and so they dreamed and painted ideas of better worlds. They believed things would only get better, that we humans would learn and progress. They believed they would hand us this better world. They did not. We read Kafka from a more pessimistic angle than did they. Our dreams are now low to the ground and the colors much duller.

Lean in close to this psalm; do you see what this protector God has busied himself with here?

First, there is God, just God. Then there is creation. Then there is Israel found in captivity. Then there is exodus. There is justice served. There is rescue "from the trampling boot." There is justice and care for everyone. And what is it that holds all of this together? It is His unrelenting love.

If God's description of what true praise constitutes is a "living praise," and if a "living praise" is to embody the things that God is concerned with, a responding to our exodus, a responding to the covering of our fall by Christ, a living that begins to move with the movements of this Christ that covers, a living that is the flesh of the concerns of God, then our living must bring rescue from the trampling boot. Justice will be our concern because it is God's concern. And what is it that causes this to well up in us? It is His unrelenting love. This is praise—taking care of everyone in time of need. It is picking up those who are marginalized and whose voices are unheard and saying, "Look! Look!" Not in calculated ways to improve upon our perceived spiritual standing but because it is in us. His unrelenting love has consumed us and when we see need there seems no alternative but to respond in the fluid movements of this redeeming covering of Christ. To feel color flood back in and our heart lift from the ground with soaring dreams of the very living, breathing kingdom of God under our feet.

This is thrilling praise to God because it is what He has busied Himself with.

JUSTICE.

# PSALM 145

I lift you high in praise, my God, O my King!
and I'll bless your name into eternity.

I'll bless you every day,
and keep it up from now to eternity.

GOD is magnificent; he can never be praised enough.
There are no boundaries to his greatness.

Generation after generation stands in awe of your work;
each one tells stories of your mighty acts.

Your beauty and splendor have everyone talking;
I compose songs on your wonders.

Your marvelous doings are headline news;
I could write a book full of the details of your
greatness.

The fame of your goodness spreads across the country;
your righteousness is on everyone's lips.

GOD is all mercy and grace —
not quick to anger, is rich in love.

GOD is good to one and all;
everything he does is suffused with grace.

Creation and creatures applaud you, GOD;
     your holy people bless you.

They talk about the glories of your rule,
     they exclaim over your splendor,

Letting the world know of your power for good,
     the lavish splendor of your kingdom.

Your kingdom is a kingdom eternal;
     you never get voted out of office.

GOD always does what he says,
     and is gracious in everything he does.

GOD gives a hand to those down on their luck,
     gives a fresh start to those ready to quit.

All eyes are on you, expectant;
     you give them their meals on time.

Generous to a fault,
     you lavish your favor on all creatures.

Everything GOD does is right —
     the trademark on all his works is love.

GOD's there, listening for all who pray,
     for all who pray and mean it.

He does what's best for those who fear him —
     hears them call out, and saves them.

GOD sticks by all who love him,
     but it's all over for those who don't.

My mouth is filled with GOD's praise.
Let everything living bless him,
bless his holy name from now to eternity!

I met my best friend, Michael Knight, in junior high while break dancing one day at recess. We bonded over "Electric Boogaloo" and the fact that he had the same name as that guy on TV who drove the coolest car ever. We were inseparable, Huckleberry Friends, all the way through high school. I spent every afternoon that I wasn't grounded at his house. His family became my family. We jumped on his trampoline. We drank Tang. We shared the ritual that was *Ferris Bueller's Day Off* after school each afternoon. I would belaboringly attempt to quote the lines that made us laugh, but I always muddled them up, as Michael would point out, and he would then proceed to deliver the line correctly and properly, with spot-on inflection and cadence, belittlingly explicating to me how "timing is everything."

There were lessons to be learned at Michael Knight's house in the afternoons after school. His dad taught us about girls. He said, "You'll know when you find her. When I met your mom I thought she was better than sliced bread." This talk of sliced bread was quite baffling to us, so we inquired of him what meaning was intended by this breaded word picture and why he spoke in such riddled analogy. He explained that loaves of bread had not always come presliced. This was huge news, and it became abundantly clear how such metaphor applied to Michael's mother. His dad then went into a lengthy dissertation involving more metaphor, including some alphabetical reference to her being everything "from A to Z" to him. I also hazily recall something related to the breathing of air, like "she's my oxygen" or some such life-vitality clause, but we were young and our attention span terrifically tiny and we really had to "get inside to watch Ferris."

On first glance, Psalm 145 seems fairly static. There is no plot building in intensity from beginning to end. It seems like you could put these verses in just about any order without loss or degradation in meaning. What seems to be articulated here is that Yahweh shelteringly rules and that this truth can be relied upon. But something is lost in translation. In Hebrew, this psalm is an acrostic.[28] It is a poem whose order must not change, as order is the point. It begins with the first letter of the alphabet and then follows sequentially with the second letter and continues on through the end. There is meaning in this order. From A to Z, Yahweh holds things together.

There is a resizing needed. There is a needed resizing of our selves. A shrinking from our consuming "me, me, me," A-to-Z centrality that so typically defines our living. And there is a need for the resizing of God. A shifting of realities. A turning of our gaze to the ultimate reality that is God. GOD, GOD, GOD, everywhere we look—GOD. He is the beginning. He is the end. He is everything in between.

 PSALM 146

Hallelujah!
   O my soul, praise GOD!
   All my life long I'll praise GOD,
   singing songs to my God as long as I live.

Don't put your life in the hands of experts
   who know nothing of life, of salvation life.
   Mere humans don't have what it takes;
   when they die, their projects die with them.
   Instead, get help from the God of Jacob,
   put your hope in GOD and know real blessing!
   GOD made sky and soil,
   sea and all the fish in it.
   He always does what he says —
   he defends the wronged,
   he feeds the hungry.
   GOD frees prisoners —
   he gives sight to the blind,
   he lifts up the fallen.
   GOD loves good people, protects strangers,
   takes the side of orphans and widows,
   but makes short work of the wicked.

GOD's in charge — always.
   Zion's God is God for good!
   Hallelujah!

I've only been angry at the rest of the human race on two occasions. Well three, but only twice was I Really Angry.[29]

Now, I know we've done some pretty atrocious things to one another at different moments throughout history, so I don't want to appear trite or oblivious to horrific events that are part of our collective experience when sharing my two moments of anger with you. I am not ignoring the wars or marginalized peoples or hate crimes or so on and so on. Tragically, these moments are expected. Historically we see them as a part of the human condition. But the two moments I really lost it with you guys were completely unexpected.

The first time was about nine years ago. It was my first plane flight. I was quite nervous, understandably. I mean, it makes no sense, a bulk of metal floating in air. I had read about Bernoulli's Principle and lift force and all. How lift force occurs because there is more pressure below the wing than above due to its curved-on-top, flat-on-bottom shape. The faster the plane moves, the more air passes above and below the wing, resulting in a greater difference in pressure. Once the lift force is more than the weight of the airplane, the plane takes off. I had read all of this somewhere. But please, a bulk of metal floating in air? I was nervous.

It was raining outside, which added to the nerves. We boarded the plane. I had a window seat. I said hello to the elderly gentleman sitting next to me and told him it was my first time to fly. He started talking about Bernoulli and I said, "I know. Thank you very much," and began reading the emergency evacuation card. I counted the seats between the exit row and me. We taxied to the runway, the pilot announced that we were "cleared for takeoff," and seconds later I was pressed to my seat by the acceleration necessitated to create just the right amount of this so-called lift force that would be our salvation or demise.

It worked! Bernoulli's Principle worked! We climbed through the rain and then disappeared into a gray fog. Looking out the window, I could see nothing. Just gray. Gray, gray, gray, and then . . . oh my word.

We broke through the clouds and it was the most stunning

thing I'd ever seen. The sun was a brilliant orange-red just above the horizon, which was puffy white, almost ocean-like, reflecting and retaining color all at the same time. It was heavenly. I couldn't breathe, it was so gorgeous. As I sat there in complete awe I began to realize I was feeling something unexpected. I was angry. I mean really, really angry. I was mad at the old man sitting next to me. I was mad at Bernoulli. I was mad at my parents. I was mad at everyone, all of you. Why didn't you tell me? I knew scores of people who had flown. Why hadn't someone, anyone, told me it was this beautiful? Why hadn't you stopped me on the street and said, "So, so sorry, I don't know you at all, but you simply must fly in a plane on a cloudy day. It's the most beautiful moment imaginable when you finally burst through the gray. It's so peaceful and angelic up there. Here's $499—go anywhere you like, just go now!"

I was so mad!

I stopped the flight attendant as she walked by and asked, "Do you see this? Is that not incredible?"

"What?" she said.

I hated her.

I tell everyone I know about this. I tell you now. It will take your breath away. I've flown often since then. I fly most every month and some weeks every day. I always ask for a window seat. And I've grown to love airplanes and Bernoulli. There's this unique sound that you can only experience sitting in an airplane. The sound of air, this whirring hiss that itself is a tad angelic. You can cup your hands to your ears (don't quite cover them completely) and come pretty close to duplicating it. Try it. You hear that? The only way I know to describe it is "airy." It's a small bit like the sound of the sea without the ebb and flow of water meeting land. It is instead constancy—unwavering, durable, and steady. During one of my flights, I was listening to this sound and looking out the window at waves of white clouds with sunlight turning a section of them yellow and I had this image of an ocean of angels in song, and their voices were like none ever heard. English is probably not their language and for some reason in my head their voices were like the sound of air, a sound that contained all the pitches and tonal colors at once and was overwhelmingly beautiful and compelling, reflecting and retaining all at the same time.

I read this psalm and I thought of my first plane flight, how it was so indescribable and so necessary to try. I thought about familiar passages from Revelation where John is given a brief glimpse of the heavens and finds an eternally existing chorus.[30] I recalled those other creation psalms where the psalmist describes the heavens and earth as constantly telling the glories of God.[31] I began thinking about the reality that we exist to be a part of this resounding anthem. We are here just for this—all for a king. *The* King.

I must tell you this now. You would feel anger if I did not. *Salvation life* is the sweetest of living. The psalmist begs us here to pursue such soaring life, to pursue such a heavenly God rather than remain fixed to the ground, living as unredeemed humans. Read again how the psalmist attempts description of the indescribable mercies and savings of God. Read as he calls us to someplace above the gray, through the clouds to a place where there is hope and healing, where justice and mercy rule, where the King of Creation cradles the widows and the orphans and the fallen, where the blind see and goodness is champion. This is our God.

There is no love greater or more beautiful. I would stop you in the street to tell you this.

 PSALM 148

Hallelujah!
 Praise GOD from heaven,
 praise him from the mountaintops;
 Praise him, all you his angels,
 praise him, all you his warriors,
 Praise him, sun and moon,
 praise him, you morning stars;
 Praise him, high heaven,
 praise him, heavenly rain clouds;
 Praise, oh let them praise the name of GOD —
 he spoke the word, and there they were!

He set them in place
 from all time to eternity;
 He gave his orders,
 and that's it!

Praise GOD from earth,
 you sea dragons, you fathomless ocean deeps;
 Fire and hail, snow and ice,
 hurricanes obeying his orders;
 Mountains and all hills,
 apple orchards and cedar forests;
 Wild beasts and herds of cattle,
 snakes, and birds in flight;
 Earth's kings and all races,
 leaders and important people,
 Robust men and women in their prime,

and yes, graybeards and little children.

Let them praise the name of GOD —
*   it's the only Name worth praising.*
His radiance exceeds anything in earth and sky;
he's built a monument — his very own people!
Praise from all who love GOD!
Israel's children, intimate friends of GOD.
Hallelujah!

The human condition hangs in the air and drips from the walls in hospitals. When I am in a hospital I always breathe through my nose.

Conversations overheard at a hospital while standing in the hall of the maternity ward on May 11, 2004, Mother's Day:

Room 3012: "There are no words. You don't know where you'll find the strength but somehow you do. It was a tragic accident. It was nothing we did wrong; it was nothing you did wrong. I don't know how to help you; please let me know how I can help you. I don't know what to do."

The next room over:

"He's beautiful. Oh my God. I love you so much. I love you so much."

Death and Life are so close together. Our fallen-ness has made it so.

The Statue of Liberty, the Washington Monument, the Jefferson Memorial, the Lincoln Memorial, the Vietnam Memorial, Mount Rushmore, Arlington National Cemetery—when we think of monuments, we think of these things erected from steel and stone. We think of chiseled words that last and inspire, things of remembrance. Monuments wish to hold something in front of us. They are the freezings of moments we ought not leave, our attempts at permanence, our efforts to build a durable history that only erosion, acid rain, vandals, or terrorists can eliminate. They are the things we come back to, to touch and recall an instant, an era, a person, a victory, a slaughter, a hero or martyr.

The children of Israel were constantly building monuments to remind them of Yahweh's intervenings. My Strong's concordance lists more than 320 Scripture references to erecting altars. A deliverance here, an exodus there, and a piling of stones to remember. Yet despite all of these reminders, there was still need for more, something more impervious to short-term memories, something more enduring, something more majestic, more strikingly splendid. There was still forgetfulness and unshakeable uncertainty about whether God's intervention and ruling would continue.

Here in this psalm we are told of a monument God Himself has built. This is one monument we can look to that did not erupt from the dreamings of our own heads or the workings of our human hands. It was erected by God to bring us ready remembrance of His faithfulness, of who He is, of what He has done and will do.

It is His very people. It is you and I. We see this God-crafted monument every time we look each other in the eye, and we remember that He has not left us for a moment. I see in your life and you in mine what He has brought us through, and there are no vandals or erosive elements that can ply their corrosive actions upon this constantly nascent memorial.

 # PSALM 150

Hallelujah!
  Praise God in his holy house of worship,
  praise him under the open skies;
  Praise him for his acts of power,
  praise him for his magnificent greatness;
  Praise with a blast on the trumpet,
  praise by strumming soft strings;
  Praise him with castanets and dance,
  praise him with banjo and flute;
  Praise him with cymbals and a big bass drum,
  praise him with fiddles and mandolin.
  Let every living, breathing creature praise GOD!
  Hallelujah!

There are songs that won't let you out of the car. There aren't a lot, but there are too many. I've wished there were fewer. Like when one of these magically enchanting songs would come on right after I pulled up to a convenience store. Four minutes of sitting in a parking space would pass before I could move, and I found myself equally inspired and troubled by my incapacity. If there were very many more of these function-depriving songs, we would be collectively incapable of enjoying such modern conveniences as radio for fear of this incapacitation. We would be forced to carefully load our iPods with songs that permit us to come and go as we please rather than glue us to our seats with arm outstretched, fingers hovering hesitantly on the volume knob, powerless to turn it off. Parking lots would be full of incessantly idling cars and relentlessly bobbing heads while stores stood vacant and wanting.

There are songs that just will not let go. And they're often the ones you would least suspect. When my wife's cousin Madison (older sister to the clever little girl with the sucker) was about three, she and her sisters had been lying in bed with their mom, Sandra, watching *Annie* the movie. After it ended, Madison crawled up close to her mother and said, "Listen. Do you hear it?"

"Hear what?" Sandra asked.

"The song."

"There's no song playing. We turned it off. Just go to sleep, okay?"

"No, I hear it. I hear Annie." Madison then proceeded to climb close enough to place her ear against her mother's, their faces touching. "Here, listen."

Sandra began laughter-infused attempts at explaining to her three-year-old daughter that it was only in her head, that what she was hearing wasn't in the air; it was inside of her, playing only in memory. Madison lay back down with the unrelenting voice of Annie crooning about "tomorrow," something that would now indubitably come more slowly, what with this unavoidable racket banging around in her head.

Music is magical.

One note can express a hundred emotions, depending on its context. A single note of C can make you weep or smile or slam your hands together repeatedly according to the chords and rhythms placed around it. And a single note becomes a different note with different color depending on the room or setting where it is sounded. It resonates or fades in different ways, bouncing around or dying off. It's thrilling.

Or perhaps you're driving in your car, listening to the radio, and you hear a song for the first time and you think, *Yeah, man. I am digging this song!* or some such idiom that expresses your complete enjoyment. By the third repeat of the chorus you're mumbling along with it, singing in those universally practiced, syllabic-vowel nonwords. The next day you're in the car and the same song comes on again and your pulse quickens. You think, *Yeah, man! I love this song!* and you find yourself singing along for most of the chorus, this time with correct words and now you're only mumbling during the verses and even in the verses you're nailing a word or two here and there, especially on the obvious rhymes like *you* followed by "(mumble, mumble) sky BLUE," singing a bit behind the beat. The next day when you're in the car, the song comes on, and these words escape, "Yeah! *My* song is on!" This song that you first heard a mere two days ago suddenly somehow has become *yours*. You sing it in the shower. You sing it at work. It is in constant rotation in your head.

Music is transferable. Sounds and words and thoughts that were someone else's creation find lodging in your chest. Music speaks of universal things. Common experience. That's why your lungs swell and your eyes close and you force as much air as possible through your vocal chords whenever you encounter a song that expresses what is your life.

I discovered this at an early age. Listening to the soundtrack for *Footloose*. I would cry noiseless tears when "I'm Holding Out for a Hero" by Bonnie Tyler began to play. It's always the ones you would least suspect. It had to be the genius of the soundtrack sequence that wore me down and melted me into this pliable Bonnie putty. I would fall asleep holding my Sony cassette Walkman to the middle of my chest. (Cassettes are these things that we used to store audio information on back in the '80s. They're playing-card-sized plastic encasements surrounding reels of fragile brown tape onto which this musical information is magnetically encoded.) Lying in bed staring at the gray ceiling, silently mouthing the words, "He's gotta be strong, and he's gotta be right . . . " along with Bonnie, and feeling everything, I would exert a small amount of downward pressure, pressing the Walkman against my sternum. I hoped that as I slept, the magnetism would attach to my insides. I wanted to feel this deeply all the time.

Psalm 150 is an ideal conclusion to the Psalter, just as Psalm 1 was a brilliant start, giving argument for the praise that was to follow. Psalm 1 proposed the precondition of life lived under Torah as the predicate for praise. But here in Psalm 150 there is nothing argumentative or any basis given for when praise should commence. There are no reasons. There is just praise. Simply praise. Praise is really the sum of the psalms. Praise Him. Over and over praise Him. And here, in the finale, the period at the end of this collective psalm-sentence is unencumbered praise.

> As Israel (and the world) is obedient to torah, it becomes free for praise, which is its proper vocation, destiny, and purpose. In this light the expectation of Old Testament is not finally obedience, but adoration. The Psalter intends to lead and nurture people to such freedom that finds its proper life in happy communion that knows no restraint of convention or propriety. That is the hope for Israel and for all creation.[32]

That is the song that plays forever. That is the thing that glues you to your seat. That is what you have known forever to be *your* own. Praise of the high GOD who has been attached to your insides since the thought of life found its way into your bones. Turn it up and sing loud. Sing from inside where you believe. Sing the favorite song of creation, the song that will never let loose its hold. And lean in close to those around you, close enough for your faces to gently touch, and let them hear what plays ceaselessly inside you—the praise of our Maker.

CONCLUSION

Symptomatology

I did not try sushi until the fall of 2001. I've always been a firm believer in the eating of things once-living only after they have been cooked a great deal and that cooked cow will always taste better than barely dead fish. I also have a hair-trigger gag reflex. It is connected to my keen olfactory sense, but there is the occasional taste that sets it off as well. I have a number of friends who did not have the fortune to grow up in the sheltered lands of East Texas or with Fruit Hoops and government cheese and whose venturings into the land of gourmet food couture far exceed mine. These urbane friends have long been intent on broadening my palette by sharing their love of sushi with me. But I am the epitome of "meat and potatoes." Pizza with multiple meats is quite the exotic dish in my bucolic opinion.

Now, one particular fall evening found me and a few of these cultured friends crammed into a tiny room in the back of a little theater in Florida, and the only thing on the menu seemed to be fresh, uncooked Asian cuisine. I kicked and fussed for what was truly a necessary and unavoidable quantity of time, touting rules of temperature for served meats and the lack of well-disciplined health inspection for catering companies, but I am weak and susceptible to refined friends beating on a table while chanting my name. And so a California roll was chosen as my initiatory rite of passage into the high culture that is sushi.

"You will like it better with the wasabi sauce," said my good friend Shelley.

"With whatsa sauce?" I asked.

"Wasabi sauce. It's spicy. You like spicy, right?" she deviously asked in knowing, challenging tone. "It will cover the fishy taste. I mean, if that's what you're worried about. It's not *hot* hot . . . see . . . ," as she took a very large portion in a spoon, heaped it on a wad of rice and fish and little twigs—I was certain I saw twigs—and popped it in her mouth, grinning and chewing with total satisfaction. She swallowed.

"You can hold your nose," she said.

"Yeah? Okay," I said. And I thought, *I'm breathing in the longest breath of my life.*

I took the whole thing in and immediately I was choking or gagging or both, I'm still unsure. The bite of the wasabi had caught me off guard and this split second of vulnerability was all that was required for the air to come rushing in, begging for entrance as it tried to find route and make its way around the rice and meat and twigs—I swear I tasted twigs. The evil sauce had now found its way into my sinus cavity by way of circumventing my uvula—the small, fleshy, V-shaped extension of the soft palate that hangs above the tongue—better known as the "hangy-jangy" at the back of my throat. It had somehow leaped nefariously upward around the hangy-jangy into the nasal passageways, and now fire was in my nose. I was howling burning tears, and flaming mucus was leaking out of my nostrils and congregating on my upper lip—all of this happening at a pace too unnatural for mere food causation.

I may be overly sensitive. I make this hacking gag noise just taking out the trash. Normal people don't do this. Funeral homes and hospitals make me cry just driving by them at times, and this annoys me. And in airports I occasionally am afraid to watch other people, these spaces so full of dark and light. It's like I absorb the pain . . . the joy . . . the place is just so full of humanity and the stuff of living—the sadness of departure, the happiness of return, the heaviness of individuality—those in constant motion and those sitting quietly waiting in covert inanimateness, thinking, *If I am just still enough . . .*

It is all too present and visible to me—the mountains that are carried, the weight in the eye. If you take the time, you see it and you know, because it has been felt before. The look is recognized. I've seen it before, full and present around a bed at my wife's house in Texarkana, where her Aunt Sandra lay breathing staggered, rattling gasps as cancer won and we and her children quietly watched—I've seen it in the eyes of my Uncle Thelen asking for more morphine while lying in a hospice bed that he had ordered himself, knowingly, before the cancer had laid him in it. I watched my aunt adjust the drip and asked her why it hurt and she said she didn't really understand—I heard it in my friend Michael's voice as he recounted to me his furtive followings of his father around our town in order to catch him cheating on his mom and what it felt like the moment he saw his dad and lover embrace in a darkened downtown alleyway. . . .

And the lights go out and you think, *I can no longer see—the way is obscured by the dark* or *This is the end.*

THE ANCIENT CHINESE SECRET

Se-mi-ot-ics *n*

1. the study of signs and symbols of all kinds, what they mean, and how they relate to the things or ideas they refer to.

I bought a T-shirt in Washington, D.C. It was red. It said "Ancient Chinese Secret" on the front of it. Below this statement, it had writing, which I assumed to be Chinese. Never assume. My sushi friend Shelley was there when I picked it out. I held it up and she said, "Oh, that is soooo Crowder." I put it on that very day. I ate lunch in it sitting across from the pastors of the church where we were playing music later that evening. As I made my way across the stage, heading for our bus that was parked outside, our lighting technician stopped me and said, "Wow. You are brave."

"Yes. Well, brave how? I mean, what do you mean 'brave'?"

"The shirt. You know the secret right?"

"Well, yeah." I nervously responded in an uncertain chuckle. It is embarrassing to wear a shirt and not know what it means. "Wait, what? You mean you know Chinese? Wow. So, huh, well, what does it say? I don't know the secret. I don't know Chinese. What's the secret?"

"Oh, it's in English."

"What? No! I studied this shirt at the store like a flipping semiotician. It is most certainly not in English. That I am sure of."

"It is in English. Turn the shirt sideways, then read."

It was most definitely in English. Granted, it was intended to be cleverly hidden in ornate, faux Chinese brushstrokes, but once spotted it was unmistakable. I was wearing a shirt that said, "Go F#$@ Yourself!" It was all I could see now. How had I missed this? I am not a semiotician. I sat across from pastors eating hamburgers, laughing and smiling, while the whole time this was written on my chest!

Stuff in life happens and we try to make sense of it. So we look carefully. What could this moment, this tragedy, this weight, this mountain, this tearing, this violence, this frenzy that is life be teaching us? What is being said here? And then someone points out, "Hey, it says, 'Go F#$@ Yourself!'" and you've had it on the whole time.

Se-mi-ot-ics *n*

2. the study of identifying the ways that various symptoms indicate the disease that underlies them. (*Medical*)

The real message, the thing that is scribbled barely legible, the thing that's always there, underlying, is—we need rescue. Things aren't as they should be. When your eyes focus and this becomes visible, you can't tear your eyes from it. And you start to see that there are those all around us who wait in begging wonder. "What is wrong? I am here. I am here and I need you to notice. At times I'm waving my arms above my head, screaming it. At times I am too frightened to move, but always I am here and I want you to notice. And in the dark I am afraid. I lie with my hand on my chest waiting for the tapping to come." Things aren't as they should be. There are symptoms. You see it in my eyes. I have seen it in your eyes, too.

COME TO JESUS

To follow Jesus doesn't remove us from the stuff of life. It is not resolution. It is tension and journey. First John 2:6 states, "Whoever claims to live in him must walk as Jesus did" (NIV). Jesus was in the world, engaged, alive, involved, making a difference. To follow Him, we must do the same. His prayer for us in John 17 is "Not that you take them out of the world . . . " and "As you sent me into the world, I have sent them into the world" (verses 15,18, NIV). This is what God has done for us. He has come into our condition. He has come to bring us back. He has come and embraced us. He has come and covered us in Himself. Watch this Christ. Watch as He is accused of being a drunkard, of associating with tax collectors. Watch as He brings healing to the afflicted, love to prostitutes, forgiveness to sinners. Watch as He climbs the hill bearing His destruction on His back. Watch as blood and water flow. Watch as salvation comes to us all. Watch as glory ascends to come again. Watch and fall in love with a God who does not resolve, whose rescue is never-ending. Whose prayer is that you would be that rescue. Who sends you to be that rescue. Be courageous. Even as you stand there hiding in the bushes, shaking to the bottom of your toes, frightened of what's to follow, what consequences will come of it, know that evil will not prevail. That you are not alone. That you bring the kingdom of God and there is hope. There is hope always. And others will walk out of dark places and see you standing there, arms outstretched, given completely to this hope.

Praise is response. Praise happens when there is revelation, and there is revelation waiting for us around every bend, in places we would not suspect. Our task is to live with eyes wide open to God's greatness because when we see the imprint of the Creator, our insides will swell with devotion, our hearts will erupt with thankfulness. You will live, breathe, and radiate praise. The habit isn't in learning *how* to praise; it is in reminding yourself *who* to praise. It is a remembering of who you are. It is a remembering of your identity. Praise is redeemed and redefined with rescue. When you have been found by grace, your identity is swallowed in Christ. You are enveloped by Him, clothed in His merciful sacrifice. To live in this remembrance is to bring awareness of Christ into your every encounter. In this awareness you bring His embrace to the things you embrace.

YOU ARE HERE

There is a sign in my favorite restaurant, *1424,* which happens to be located directly across the street from my house, that hangs by the bar and states, in black letters on a pale-yellow background, "You Are Here." I call often for takeout. I pretend that they are my residential kitchen staff that just so happens to cook the most flavorful foods on the planet. The chef's name is Bill, and he knows exactly how I like my pork tenderloin. We have never discussed it; he just knows. He's always known. And as I wait for my order to be packed in white Styrofoam and placed in a plastic bag for transport, I sit at the bar and read, "You Are Here," and it brings a comfort and solidity to things. You often hear or encounter inspirational art convincing you to live as if today is the last, to engage each moment as if it were all we had, but usually this is married to the idea that it is. That *this is it.* There is nothing more than now. All we get is what we suck out of this moment. But I disagree. I read, "You Are Here," and I am equally inspired to be fully present in this moment, but it is not because that is all I have but because I am bringing something more. I am bringing the very kingdom of God. I read, "You Are Here," and I, ignoring the dramatic punctuation of finality, think, "The kingdom of God is sitting at this bar, waiting to bring something better."

We are to be rescue. We are to be redemption. We are to carry the story of God to the ones waiting. To the ones with their hands on their chest, begging you to notice that things aren't right. And this is praise. You are the note sounding in a thousand different rooms. There are chords and reflective surfaces around you. There is context.

Sometimes life comes at us with the delicacy of a sunset, and other times it comes with the rawness of sushi and the bitter bite of wasabi. Sometimes the tears will be because you cannot stand empty-eyed in the presence of such beauty and sometimes they will be full of fire, but notice/know this: *You are here.* You Are Here! You are here and you are not alone.

Look me in the eyes. Can you feel the fabric on your skin? It is woven from the threads of love. Pay attention to the way it folds around you, sense its softness, brush the hair of your arms as you lift them toward the heavens in unencumbered declaration.

It is the coverings of rescue that you feel. It is a flood. It is an ocean. It is a sea that has no bottom, for there is no end to it. To be fully present in the rescue and recreation of Christ is to embrace what God does for us, and this is the best thing we can do for Him.

APPENDIX A[33]

fig. 1

fig. 8   fig. 19

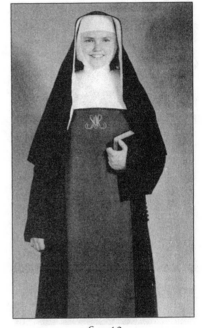

fig. 29   *fig. 40*

fig. 50   fig. 63

fig. 66   *fig.* 74

fig. 75   fig. 84

fig. 88　　　　　　　　　　fig. 96

fig. 100   *fig. 113*

fig. 121   fig. 136

fig. 145   fig. 146

fig. 148   *fig. 150*

APPENDIX B³⁴

READ. THINK. PRAY. LIVE.

There's an ancient practice called *lectio divina* (or "spiritual reading") that has been used for centuries to [help readers discover revelation through Scripture]. The space here is way too short to cover everything, but here's a quick intro. If you want to learn more about it, you can find books or go on-line and look into it. Basically there are four components that make up *lectio*: reading, thinking, praying, and living. Sounds easy, but it takes some practice to get into the groove.

READ.

Sounds easy, doesn't it? But this probably takes the most practice. We live in a culture that places significant value on time and convenience, and this first practice is anything but speedy. To truly read [Scripture], you've got to soak yourself in it.

Have you ever been to the ocean? Have you ever been *in* the ocean? Not just pulling up in a car, taking your shoes off, and sticking your big toe in the water. Have you ever *immersed* yourself in the ocean? When you do that, it's almost as if a whole new world opens up to you. You see and feel and taste and hear things that you never could have just walking along the beach—you experience things hidden from the spectators on the beach. It's the same thing when you come to the [Scriptures]. When you *immerse* yourself in them, a whole new world opens up.

As usual, [Scripture] really says it best:

Place these words on your hearts. Get them deep inside you. Tie them on your hands and foreheads as a reminder. . . . Talk about them wherever you are, sitting at home or walking in the street; talk about them from the time you get up in the morning until you fall into bed at night. Inscribe them on the doorposts and gates of your cities so that you'll live a long time. (Deuteronomy 11)

How can a young person live a clean life?
    By carefully reading the map of your Word.
    I'm single-minded in pursuit of you;
    don't let me miss the road signs you've posted.
        (Psalm 119)

Eugene describes it this way:

First, it is important simply to read, leisurely and thoughtfully. We need to get a feel for the way these stories and songs, these prayers and conversations, these sermons and visions, invite us into this large, large world in which the invisible God is behind and involved in everything visible, and illuminates what it means to live here — really live, not just get across the street.

As we read, and the longer we read, we begin to 'get it' — we are in conversation with God. We find ourselves listening and answering in matters that most concern us: who we are, where we came from, where we are going, what makes us tick, the texture of the world and the communities we live in, and — most of all — the incredible love of God among us, doing for us what we cannot do for ourselves.

Through reading the Bible, we see that there is far more to the world, more to us, more to what we see and more to what we don't see — more to everything! — than we had ever dreamed, and that this 'more' has to do with God.

This is new for many of us, a different sort of

book — a book that reads us even as we read it. We are used to picking up and reading books for what we can get out of them: information we can use, inspiration to energize us, instructions on how to do something or other, entertainment to while away a rainy day, wisdom that will guide us into better living. These things can and do take place when reading the Bible, but the Bible is given to us in the first place simply to invite us to make ourselves at home in the world of God, God's word and world, and become familiar with the way God speaks and the ways in which we answer him with our lives.

What's up with that? "A book that reads us even as we read it"? That's a pretty strange statement at first glance. What other book can you say that about? What magazine has ever read you as you read it? What you hold in your hands, however, contains our collective stories. Each of us can find little glimpses of ourselves in these pages. The people in the [Scriptures] are a whole lot like you, and a lot of them were far from perfect. We need to open our eyes and see what God would have each of us understand about ourselves.

So you can see that it's not the same thing as reading the latest issue of your favorite magazine or a Shakespearian sonnet. There's something different here—something that the creator of the universe wants to tell you and wants you to understand about him and yourself. By jumping into [Scripture], you open your eyes to God's world and see how he includes you in his story.

THINK.

After reading, the next step is to really think about what [Scripture] is saying. This may seem obvious, but there is a difference between letting your mind wander over a few verses or chapters and trying to figure out what it means.

Have you ever been to the Grand Canyon? There are some people who drive up to the edge, jump out of their cars, poke around for a few minutes, maybe take a few pictures, and then head off to the gift shop to buy T-shirts or snow globes to take to their friends back home.

There are others who spend an entire day seated quietly away from the noisy tourists, simply watching from their own private spot. That may sound boring, but to some, the Grand Canyon is a place of incredible beauty and power—one quick look isn't enough. They want to soak it in. And those people will often come back year after year, to sit in that same spot—and every time, they see a different show.

You can think about the [Scriptures] in the same way. You can read a sentence or two, quickly decide what they mean and make a mental check next to them, and then head off to the gift shop.

Or, you can spend days and weeks (or even months) meditating on what a particular passage is really talking about—turning it over in your mind, reflecting on it, soaking it in. You can consider what those words mean against the changing backdrop of real life—of your life. You can begin to perceive the importance and subtle meanings of each word that's found its way from God to you. You can learn to identify the sound of God's voice as you get to know him better. You can think about them from all sorts of different viewpoints, even putting yourself in the shoes of the characters you're reading about. You can certainly ask the Author to help you soak it all in: "With your very own hands you formed me; now breathe your wisdom over me so I can understand you" (Psalm 119). God and his thoughts are so complex, with so many aspects and perspectives, that you can come back to his words again and again.

This way of thinking about [Scripture] is talked about in a number of places in the Bible. Perhaps the best example can be found in Psalm 1: "You thrill to God's Word. You chew on it day and night." It's not like a meal that you gulp down before you head out the door to do what you really want to do.

This is the five-star meal that you savor—with your mind, your heart, and your soul. It's the main event, and you have the opportunity to spend hours at the table relishing each bite.

> I ponder every morsel of wisdom from you,
> I attentively watch how you've done it.
> I relish everything you've told me of life,
> I won't forget a word of it. . . .
> My soul is starved and hungry, ravenous! —
> insatiable for your nourishing commands. . . .
> Your words are so choice, so tasty;
> I prefer them to the best home cooking.
> (Psalm 119)

PRAY.

You've read the text. You've spent time thinking. Now comes prayer. The kind of prayer we're talking about goes beyond merely asking for things—although there's a time for that, and God even tells us to do that often. But in this process of *lectio divina*, there's a time when you need to acknowledge what God is saying to you. Did God reveal something new about who he is? Did he reveal something about who you are in his eyes? Is he asking you to think about someone in a different light? Talk to God about it. Ask God to show you more about what you've just read: "Help me understand these things inside and out so I can ponder your miracle-wonders" (Psalm 119). Don't just read through [Scripture] and breeze through the prayer part. Go beyond the usual "thanks for this or that, help me to be a better person" routine. Have a *conversation* with God. He *wants* to do that with you.

These conversational prayers that flow out of what you read may be less about you and more about God. Your focus may shift away from yourself and toward your creator.

Don't be afraid to pray about a passage more than once—in fact, that's a good thing. You may want to pray with a different focus at different times—talking to God about what you're learning, thanking him for the truth in the passage, asking God questions, asking him to show you how to make the words real in your life, asking forgiveness for what you see in yourself after reading, just listening . . . There are a lot of ways to go about prayer.

As you continue on in this process, trying it several times, you may be thinking, *Praying over the same part of Scripture seems pretty redundant. I'm doing the same thing over and over and over again*—and you'd be right. The point of all of this is not to be doing something new at each step. The point is to focus more intentionally on God and what he's communicating to you through this process.

Think about it this way: If you have a friend who constantly asks you for things but never really wants to listen to you, how deep will your relationship go? Sometimes we forget that God has a personality and wants to engage us at a deeper level. Let prayer be a time that you come to savor and look forward to. Allow this to be a time in which God speaks to you and you actively seek him. An audible voice may not come booming out of the clouds, but many things will be revealed to you through this process—about God, about reality, and about you.

LIVE.

This is where these words begin to shape life. Jesus was the first one to *become* God's words in the flesh.

> *The Word became flesh and blood,*
> *and moved into the neighborhood.*
> *We saw the glory with our own eyes,*
> *the one-of-a-kind glory,*
> *like Father, like Son,*
> *Generous inside and out,*
> *true from start to finish. (John 1)*

God's word by its very nature changes us to make us like Christ: "God means what he says. What he says goes. His powerful Word is sharp as a surgeon's scalpel, cutting through everything, whether doubt or defense, laying us open to listen and obey" (Hebrews 4). If you read what God has written, think about it, pray through it, but don't allow it to change you, you're missing a big point. James puts it this way:

> Don't fool yourself into thinking that you are a listener when you are anything but, letting the Word go in one ear and out the other. Act on what you hear! Those who hear and don't act are like those who glance in the mirror, walk away, and two minutes later have no idea who they are, what they look like.
>
> But whoever catches a glimpse of the revealed counsel of God — the free life! — even out of the corner of his eye, and sticks with it, is no distracted scatterbrain but a man or woman of action. That person will find delight and affirmation in the action. (James 1)

Imagine going on a dream date—the right person, the right clothes, the right food, the right conversation . . . perfect! You excuse yourself from the table, take a look at the mirror in the restroom, and . . . uh-oh, not so perfect. *Aaah! How long has that been in my teeth? Did my date notice? How could someone not notice?* Then, having seen yourself clearly, you walk back out and sit down at the table, with a piece of your dinner adorning your teeth in all its glory.

The same kind of thing happens when you read the Bible and do nothing. Not only is the sin that you leave in place ugly and damaging, but it also stands in the way of your relationship with God—in a much bigger way than something hanging off your face. For God to share his mind and his heart with you, only to have you do nothing about it, implies more than a self-destructive choice. Instead of doing what God says, you have chosen yourself as master, as god.

The great part is that God doesn't leave you alone. He doesn't show you how lost you are and then leave you high and dry. God helps you live the way he wants. Like Paul told the Philippians, "Be energetic in your life of salvation, reverent and sensitive before God. That energy is God's energy, an energy deep within you, God himself willing and working at what will give him the most pleasure" (Philippians 2).

The amazing thing about reading the [Scriptures] is that as you spend time with God, this reading becomes part of you. Like the way relationships with other humans change us and shape our lives, our relationship with God changes us on a much larger scale. In *lectio divina,* reading, thinking, and praying come together within us, become part of us. . . .

This offers us a tremendous sense of freedom—from our futile and determined attempts to save ourselves by being "good enough," from the captivity of sin that makes us slaves. In Matthew 11, Jesus says, "Walk with me and work with me—watch how I do it. Learn the unforced rhythms of grace. I won't lay anything heavy or ill-fitting on you. Keep company with me and you'll learn to live freely and lightly."

The Bible and its message help you leave behind things that seem to offer pleasure (like living for yourself) but fail and leave you empty. God's word does more than that. You find true life. Jesus says in John, "I came so they can have real and eternal life, more and better life than they ever dreamed of" (John 10). Jesus himself *is* life (John 14). So don't miss this: When you live the Word, you truly *live.*

APPENDIX C

Behold Nunzilla

a. Nunzilla side view

b. Nunzilla front view

Nunzilla's actual pattern of travel

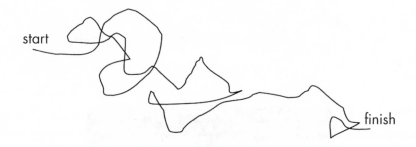

Instructions for optimal travel length:
1. Experiment with counterweight.
2. Surface selection is paramount. Although the seduction of paraffin wax is great, we recommend polished aluminum.
3. Experiments involving gaffer's tape for heightened aerodynamics have not been helpful.
4. Nunzilla has been known to respond to the recordings of David Hasselhoff or Gagaku, an ancient form of Japanese classical music.
5. Do not look directly at Nunzilla!
6. Dim lighting is suggested.
7. Do not wear orange.

APPENDIX D

NOTES

1. Derrida, Jacques (1930–), French philosopher, whose work originated the school of deconstruction, a strategy of analysis that has been applied to literature, linguistics, philosophy, law, and architecture. ("Derrida, Jacques," *Microsoft® Encarta® Encyclopedia 99.* © 1993-1998 Microsoft Corporation. All rights reserved.)

2. "Habit," *Microsoft® Encarta® Encyclopedia 99.* © 1993-1998 Microsoft Corporation. All rights reserved.

3. "Will (philosophy and psychology)," *Microsoft® Encarta® Encyclopedia 99.* © 1993-1998 Microsoft Corporation. All rights reserved.

4. Noun 1. Bundle of His—a bundle of modified heart muscle that transmits the cardiac impulse from the atrioventricular node to the ventricles, causing them to contract. Thefreedictionary.com, s.v. "Bundle of His."

5. "Fly on the Wall," *Conversations: A Journal for Authentic Transformation,* 1, Spring 2003, www.conversationsjournal .com.

6. Richard J. Foster, *Celebration of Discipline* (San Francisco: HarperSanFrancisco, 1988), p. 8.

7. Dictionary.com, s.v. "habit."

8. Speaking of *Breakfast at Tiffany's,* I'm not sure if there has ever been a better line written in any song than "my huckleberry friend" in Henry Mancini's "Moon River." It kills me. When Audrey sang it, hanging so coolly out of her apartment window with her guitar, I knew what she was feeling. Here, behold:

   Moon river
   Wider than a mile
   I'm crossing you in style some day
   Oh dream maker you heart breaker

Wherever you're going I'm going your way.

Two drifters off to see the world
There's such a lot of world to see
We're after that same rainbow's end
Waiting round the bend my huckleberry friend
Moon river and me

9. Elizabeth Kuhns, *The Habit: A History of the Clothing of Catholic Nuns* (New York: Doubleday, 2003), pp. 3, 6, 7.

10. Kuhns, p. 7.

11. Paraphrased from Romans 12, *The Message*.

12. Walter Brueggemann, *The Message of the Psalms* (Minneapolis: Augsburg Fortress, 1984), p. 11.

13. Brueggemann, p. 16.

14. See Brueggemann, p. 17.

15. Brueggemann, pp. 38-39.

16. http://hubblesite.org/newscenter/newsdesk/archive/releases/1999/25, "Magnificent Details in a Dusty Spiral Galaxy," credit Hubble Heritage Team 1999.

17. http://www.earthsky.org/scienceqs.

18. "The Ballad of Gilligan's Isle," by Sherwood Schwartz and George Wyle © 1964, 1966 EMI U Catalog Inc. Copyrights Renewed. All rights controlled by EMI U Catalog Inc. (Publishing) and Warner Bros. Publications Inc. (Print). All rights reserved. Used by permission. Warner Bros. Publications U.S. Inc., Miami, FL 33014.

19. I must make note as I have made such vast claims regarding smoked meats. To be completely truthful, my favorite barbecue is not the place with the pistol, although the pistol place does have the best buffet you will ever carry a tray through. I had to say such things because a pistol smoker makes a better story. In truth, if you wish to taste the best brisket

on the planet, you will need to head down Franklin Avenue
in a southerly direction, away from the pistol. Take a right
on Valley Mills Drive. Follow Valley Mills exactly 2.7 miles.
Uncle Dan's is located on the corner of Valley Mills and Lake
Air Drive. Ask for Dan. Tell him I sent you and then order the
chopped brisket sandwich or the Texas Tater. I would insist
on the Texas Tater but it will dwell with you for days and I
don't want the blame to lie here.

Michna's Barbecue (Pistol Smoker)
2803 Franklin Avenue
Waco TX

Uncle Dan's Authentic Texas Rib House
1001 Lake Air Drive
Waco TX

20. *The New Oxford Annotated Bible* (New York: Oxford
University Press, 1973), p. 702.

21. Daniel Cresswell, as quoted in *The Treasury of David*, by
Charles Spurgeon (Nashville: Nelson, 1998), http://bible.
crosswalk.com/Commentaries/TreasuryofDavid/tod.cgi?book
=ps&chapter=066&verse=001.

22. Brueggemann, p. 67.

23. Brueggemann, pp. 78-81.

24. *Baker's Evangelical Dictionary of Biblical Theology,* s.v. "God,
Names of."

25. *Baker's Evangelical Dictionary of Biblical Theology,* s.v. "God,
Names of."

26. Gelatin is made of gross stuff that you do not want to eat.
Don't ever ask anyone about it. You are better off not knowing. My life sans Jello is lacking, and I wish yours to be full
and free.

27. Eugene H. Peterson, "Introduction: Genesis," *The Message:
The Bible in Contemporary Language* (Colo. Springs, Colo.:
NavPress, 2002), p. 19.

28. Brueggemann, p. 28.

29. The second time I was Really Angry with you was when I was in Hawaii and tasted the pineapple there. Why didn't you tell me?

30. See Revelation 5:11-13; 19:1-8.

31. See Psalm 69; 96.

32. Brueggemann, p. 167.

33. Kuhns, pp. 171-186.

34. Appendix B reprinted with permission. Eugene H. Peterson, *The Message Remix: The Bible in Contemporary Language* (Colorado Springs, Colo.: NavPress, 2003), pp. 16-23.

INDEX

AUTHOR

DAVID CROWDER is the pastor of music and arts at University Baptist Church in Waco, Texas, where he lives with his wife, Toni. They have no pets, although he does like some animals. There is nothing to see out the window through which he is so intently staring. He is also a small part of the fabulous rock-and-roll extravagance known as David Crowder*Band on the music recording label Sixstepsrecords/EMI CMG. This is his first book. (He is writing this spiel in third person because he is told this is the way of writing such spiels.)

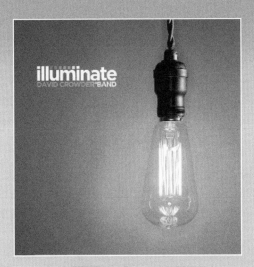

own your faith

Ask Me Anything
J. Budziszewski
978-1-57683-650-7

Dr. Budziszewski (aka Professor Theophilus) offers his expert opinion to help you achieve personal insight about the most controversial and confusing topics of our time.

Renovation of the Heart:
An Interactive Student Edition
Dallas Willard
978-1-57683-730-6

With easy-to-understand examples, review questions, and explanations of key words, learn how to understand one of the most complicated and important lessons of life: putting on the character of Christ.

To order copies, call NavPress at 1-800-366-7788
or log on to www.navpress.com.